KU-713-545

INTRODUCTION

A *New Deal for Carers* is about the needs of carers – the many people in this country who look after a relative or friend who, because of disability, illness or old age, cannot manage at home without help. The work is based on discussions with nearly two hundred people around the country, working in many different organisations and in many different capacities, all concerned with some aspect of carers and caring. We were given not only a very warm response but much more time than could reasonably have been expected. It is obvious that we could not have written this work without their contribution.

There are about six million carers in Great Britain with about 1.7 million caring for someone in the same household. In 1986 the Family Policy Studies Centre estimated the value of some of the care provided by 1.3 million carers at between £5.1 and £7.3 billions. They argued that if 10% of these carers were to stop providing care it would cost £1.1 billions in increased public expenditure. (1986 price levels).

The people they care for are diverse and the services they require in order to care for them vary enormously. While it is true that recognition and support for carers have increased in recent years, community care policies and financial restraint can put them at risk of exploitation.

In this work we have set out to identify and state the needs which carers have in common. This statement of needs provides the basis for developing policies and practices that will give a new deal for carers.

The changes involved in this are not easy but with energy and a sense of

AIMS AND CONTENT

purpose and vision they can be made, as we have seen in different parts of the country. Not all require new resources. Some rely on a change of attitude or a commitment to monitor and review existing services or collaborate more effectively. There are many things which can help provide recognition to carers. For example, it can help regularly to consider the impact any service changes may have on carers. It can help to increase consultation and encourage consumer involvement. It can help to work with the family as well as the individual client. All these things allow carers to be treated as equal partners in developing a strategy of community care instead of as supplicants in the queue for resources.

A New Deal for Carers draws together ideas from all over the country in a format that can be used by workers at all levels to review their current policy and practice and develop a better service for carers. It is based around '*Carers' Needs — a 10 Point Plan for Carers*' which sets out essential requirements that must be met if carers are to lead a reasonable and worthwhile life with the person they care for (see page 5). Each of these needs is then explored in detail in the following ten chapters. Each chapter consists of:

- explanations and discussions of the carers' needs
- suggestions for reviewing the way the need is being met locally
- ideas for practical action at local level to meet the need more effectively
- ideas for developing policy, organisation and training that will ensure the need is properly met
- examples from different parts of the country of how new initiatives are being developed

THE CARING ROLE

Caring is a job, but a job with a difference. It has no fixed hours and no wages. There are no qualifying exams, no queue of applicants and no clear contract. It arrives through and takes place within a relationship. Carers are daughters, husbands, mothers, sometimes friends looking after another person who is unable to manage alone. These relationships may be very good or regrettably poor. Many are a mixture of the two. They are likely, at some point, to have involved love and conflict, giving and taking. The fact that caring takes place within a relationship gives an added meaning to the tasks that carers do. Many do them with great love, generosity and loyalty. Indeed, people do not typically identify themselves as 'carers' at all, but as 'looking after Mum'. The extended duties are seen as part and parcel of their family roles. But other carers feel trapped by the lack of alternatives, by the indifference of relatives and friends or by the absence of official provision. They act out of a sense of duty but yearn for

KING ALFRED'S COLLEGE
WINCHESTER

Library: 01962 827306

To be returned on or before the day
marked below, subject to recall

2 8 NOV 2005

1 2 DEC 2006

0 1 OCT 2007

1 3 NOV 2007

- 4 NOV 2008

- 2 DEC 2008

WITHDRAWN FROM
THE LIBRARY

UNIVERSITY OF
WINCHESTER

KA 0193289 6

CONTENTS

KING ALFRED'S COLLEGE
WINCHESTER

649.8
RIC   019932896

more support, relief and others to share their responsibilities. There may also be conflicts of interest between carers and the people they care for. For example, a daughter looking after her chronically ill mother may very much need a break. The mother may resent any suggestion that she is a burden and not wish to change her routine in any way.

Most carers are women but there are also many male carers, and individual circumstances vary enormously. There are differences in the severity of the condition of the person cared for, the prognosis, in the stigma attached to the condition, and in the quality of the relationship of carer and the person they cared for.

Some carers are elderly or frail themselves. Some are children caring for a parent who is disabled. Some carers look after more than one person. Black and ethnic minority carers, who have the same needs as other carers, often have added difficulties in obtaining the help they need. Services can seem inaccessible and inappropriate to many carers. Economic circumstances, housing conditions, the extent to which they have some support and feel part of their local community all may ease or compound the problems of individual carers.

The tasks of caring can be tiring, restricting and even potentially dangerous. Lifting, for example, is a frequent cause of injury. Many carers are unable to go out to work and some cannot get out of the house at all. But it is often the emotional side which creates the greatest strain. Feelings of resentment over the restrictions imposed, anguish over the way a loved person has changed, guilt about all the help not given can create sizeable tensions. Where the relationship was never very good in the first place, carers are likely to experience particular anxiety and conflict about their role.

People often find themselves immersed in the role of carer, with little or no chance to review their position and consider whether it is what they want to do. Once acquired, the role is exceedingly difficult to shed. All the pressures − both external and, perhaps more important, internal − are on the carer to care.

Yet, for the most part, the services carers receive are only marginal to their lives. Few carers see the statutory sector as providing a backbone to their support or as a partner in caring. Nor do many carers get much help from anyone else. It is this situation that needs to change.

CARERS NEEDS − A 10-POINT PLAN FOR CARERS

Carers are people who are looking after elderly, ill or disabled relatives or friends who cannot manage at home without help. They may be the parents of a child with a mental handicap, a husband whose wife has a physical disability or a daughter looking after her frail elderly mother.

Carers come from all racial, ethnic and religious backgrounds. Their circumstances vary enormously, with the severity of the condition of the person cared for, their economic circumstances and the overall help and support available. The majority of carers are women and many carry out the tasks of caring completely on their own.

Carers are deeply concerned about the needs of the people they care for; services need to be planned for and with them.

Carers need

1 **Recognition of their contribution** and of their own needs as individuals in their own right;

2 **Services tailored to their individual circumstances**, needs and views, through discussions at the time help is being planned;

3 **Services which reflect an awareness of differing racial, cultural and religious backgrounds** and values, equally accessible to carers of every race and ethnic origin;

4 **Opportunities for a break**, both for short spells (an afternoon) and for longer periods (a week or more), to relax and have time to themselves;

5 **Practical help** to lighten the tasks of caring, including domestic help, home adaptions, incontinence services and help with transport;

6 **Someone to talk to** about their own emotional needs, at the outset of caring, while they are caring and when the caring task is over;

7 **Information** about available benefits and services as well as how to cope with the particular condition of the person cared for;

8 **An income which covers the costs of caring** and which does not preclude carers taking employment or sharing care with other people;

9 **Opportunities to explore alternatives to family care** both for the immediate and the long-term future;

10 **Services designed through consultation** with carers, at all levels of policy planning.

Voluntary organisations who have endorsed this statement of need are:
Age Concern England
Alzheimers Disease Society
Association of Crossroads Care Attendant Schemes
Carers National Association
Contact a Family
Greater London Association for Disabled People (GLAD)
National Schizophrenia Fellowship

'Carers Needs — a 10 Point Plan for Carers' is available as a separate leaflet for use by carers and workers. For details contact Book Sales, King's Fund Centre, 126 Albert Street, London NW1 7NF.

A New Deal for Carers is designed to be used by a wide range of people. It does not need to be read straight through but can be dipped into and applied selectively. For example:

HOW TO USE THE BOOK

- **Front-line workers in health, social services and the voluntary sector** might use the review and action questions to assess and modify their personal practice with carers.
- **Managers in health, social services and the voluntary sector** might review the organisation of their service in the light of particular chapters or by looking at the policy suggestions throughout.
- **Policy makers** might concentrate on the statement 'Carers Needs — a 10 Point Plan for Carers', and the policy ideas to help shape proposals for relevant committees.
- **People responsible for training** may find material and ideas they can use in training sessions. They can also use the policy sections to check that existing training programmes contain an awareness of carers' needs.
- **Workers at all levels** might pick out individual chapters where they feel they lack knowledge and work through the text and questions.
- **A voluntary organisation** might discuss and then adopt 'Carers Needs — a 10 Point Plan for Carers' as the basis for a campaign.
- **Carers' organisations** may pick out examples of services they would like to press for in their locality.

Many of the issues will benefit from discussion between colleagues and between carers, workers and people needing care. It may be useful to think about existing forums where these discussions could take place or about setting up special meetings.

1

RECOGNISING CARERS' CONTRIBUTIONS

'I feel like a hermit — walled in — and the walls are closing in and getting higher and higher. Soon I believe no one will know I'm here.'

Recognition of carers' contribution and of their own needs as individuals in their own right.

DEVELOPING RECOGNITION

The contribution carers make often goes unrecognised. Services for people requiring care rarely take into account those who care for them. Policies are formulated and implemented with little or no thought to the needs of carers. Carers themselves often do not recognise their own contribution. Many drift into a caring role, hardly realising that they have done so. Some women carers in particular, may see it as wholly natural. They may not acknowledge the work as skilled and demanding and may feel little sense of pride in its accomplishment. Some begin to lose their own sense of identity as well as their confidence. This, in turn, can affect their ability to do their best for the people they care for.

Carers' contribution needs to be understood, valued and properly supported. Their needs and perspectives should be built into service thinking and planning, at the level of both policy and practice.

Real recognition of carers' contribution is likely to involve:
- changes in policy perspectives
- changes in attitude and practice
- changes in training

Changes in policy perspectives

Carers need to be considered in every activity or service. Policy-makers need to begin to 'think carers', gearing services to them as well as to people needing care. This means organising and providing services in ways that carers want and helping carers to get them (see Chapter 2). It means developing information and knowledge through surveys and consultation. It means remembering that carers look after people with differing disabilities and come from all racial, cultural and religious backgrounds (see Chapter 3). It means combining with other organisations both statutory and voluntary to discuss a forward programme.

In sum, there is a need to think through the implications of all community care policies and practices. The services provided need to complement and fit in with what can be offered at home. At the policy level, this means that decisions about future provision must take into account both short and long term effects on carers.

Changes in attitude and practice

Front line workers need to ensure that they take account of the needs of the carer as well as the person cared for. This may mean, for example, questioning discharge from hospital or consulting a carer about when and how it should take place. Some carers need help in recognising their own needs. They may need help in coming to terms with a sense of resentment at the stresses imposed or guilt that they do not do enough for the person needing care. Some may need opportunities to express negative feelings toward the person needing care or other family members who do not offer help. Carers may need to be reminded that, whatever the needs of the person cared for, they have needs too – indeed, that if these are not recognised, the person they care for may also suffer.

In practical terms, this means making time on visits to ask after the carer's welfare. This may mean going to another room, to give the carer the privacy and sense of freedom to talk. Sometimes it may mean confronting carers with their own needs: 'You look very tired, can I help you to get a break?' Recognising carers does not necessarily mean telling them they are doing a 'great job'. It may mean seeing the real stress that they are under.

Changes in training

The current emphasis in training is on resolving the problems of the person needing care. This needs to be broadened to a concern with the carer and other family members. All workers need to understand not only the difficulties carers experience but also what caring means to them. They need to learn to work with carers as partners, and to encourage them to talk about their needs. Training should also help people to work effectively with black and ethnic minority carers. Training for professional workers should explore the specific needs they could meet through such things as counselling, providing information and regular reviews of the support offered.

Training will be most effective when it is part of a broader organisational strategy. It should be a means of interpreting general policies towards carers so as to generate clear standards of good practice.

REVIEWING CURRENT PROVISION

The questions below suggest that you reflect on how carers' contributions are recognised in the provision currently made by the organisation you work for or are involved with. You may find it helpful to discuss them with a colleague.

- How are carers' contributions recognised at different levels of the service, for example
  - in policy statements and decisions?
  - in the practice of individuals?
  - in awareness and attitudes throughout the organisation?
- Think about one or two individual carers known to you
  - who recognises what they contribute?
  - how is this recognition expressed in terms of services made available to them?
  - how could each one's contributions be better recognised?

You may find it helpful to discuss these questions with a colleague and to seek the views of carers.

SUGGESTIONS FOR ACTION

Listed below are eleven suggestions for improving recognition of carers' contributions. They range from things that lie within individual control such as raising awareness and changing attitudes and practice to decisions involving policy change or allocation of resources.

- Identify those already in practice in your organisation or local area
- Identify any you would like to see implemented
- For any you would like to see implemented, think about:
  - how feasible this would be
  - who should be responsible for implementation
  - what you could do to start the process of implementation. Depending on the idea and your position this could mean anything from discussing the issue with colleagues and canvassing support to formulating a proposal for allocating resources.

- **Carers' days** and other special events can give carers recognition and at the same time help those providing services to learn more. They bring carers together and focus the attention of professionals on carers as a group. Carers' days have been held in many areas, including Evesham, Manchester and the London Borough of Camden. Such events need careful advance publicity: the wording of leaflets and posters may need to refer to 'people who are looking after a disabled person at home' or something similar, rather than 'carers'.

- **Consulting carers** by providing opportunities for them to feed their views into the policy process. This will also help carers feel valued. (See Chapter 10 for more detailed suggestions on formal and informal ways of finding out carers' opinions.)

- **A local statement** of carers needs can help put carers on the policy agenda. This could be initiated at a carers' day and later presented to the local council and health authority.

- **The establishment of a carers' worker** with responsibility for linking carers with policy-makers is an especially valuable form of recognition. Active support at senior management level is essential. One example of such a post in the statutory sector is in Sutton, where a worker has a brief to improve support for carers and to promote their interests (see box). Another example, in the voluntary sector, exists in Swindon where the Neighbourhood Care Project employs a worker to provide support, information and advocacy.

- **Improving carers' access to existing resources** by providing appropriate information, such as packs for carers or a telephone linkline, so that carers know where to go for help. (See Chapter 7 for more ideas on this.)

- **Treating carers as partners in care.** When a diagnosis is made, for instance, carers should be given as much information as possible about the likely course of the condition and consulted about what they want and feel able to do.

- **Encouraging carers to recognise their own needs** and to feel justified in having needs of their own. This means making time for the carer as well as the person requiring care.

- **Supporting the establishment of carers' support groups.** These groups offer a unique source of empathy and support, enabling carers to recognise their own value and share problems. They may be general (for all carers) or have a specific focus (such as caring for mentally ill people). Through campaigning activities, they can also play a key role in helping carers to become more effective at speaking on their own behalf. Carers should be encouraged to contact a local carers' group, where one exists. Local service providers should also make efforts to develop and sustain such groups (see Chapter 6).

- **Giving carers opportunities to step outside the caring role** and have time for themselves. This can be achieved by:

- providing respite care for short or longer periods and helping carers to use this service. Many carers are so highly accustomed to their daily routine that they fail to recognise their own need for time apart. (See Chapter 4).
- helping carers to find outlets for their own interests or people with whom they can do the things they like. Carers' groups, as well as exploring the problems of caring, can provide outings, social events and opportunities to get away.
- helping carers to gain access to the ordinary education and leisure opportunities open to all. Those providing such facilities can work with sitting services to help carers commit themselves to a regular activity. For example, in Rochdale, the Education Department has been exploring possibilities for setting up a sitting service for carers wanting to pursue education.

■ **Improving the training** of all people who work with carers and the people they care for by:

- including carers' needs as part of the main curriculum of both professional courses and induction processes for home helps, home care assistants and other people going into carers' homes.
- using the carers' development worker (where there is one) to help develop training on carers' issues.
- inviting carers to contribute to training sessions. Many carers' groups are willing to provide speakers.
- providing 'on-the-job' training opportunities. One imaginative example has been devised by the local branch of the Carers National Association in Liverpool. This is a 'snakes and ladders' game, to be played by mixed teams of carers and professionals. It demonstrates how the health and welfare system looks from a carer's perspective and highlights some of the apparently random events which help or hinder progress through it.

■ **Finding out where carers are, who they are caring for, and what services they receive and need.** This could be done by:

- A broad household survey which maps out the numbers and location of carers in an area and pinpoints particular groups, such as carers of people with specific disabilities. It may be particularly important in the case of black and ethnic minority carers, who are often among the most isolated and least recognised. A survey can also be used to consult carers about their needs. (See Tameside survey, Chapter 10).
- A limited survey of the users of a particular facility or service or one group of carers. In the course of setting up the Nottingham Community Mental Handicap Teams, for instance, social workers carried out a survey of all

families containing children and adults with learning difficulties. This brought short-term help to parents and enabled them to take part in subsequent workshops to discuss specific issues. The workers involved became more aware of parents' needs and parents were able to participate in the planning of locally based services.

- Tapping into existing sources of information such as health visitors, district nurses or carers' groups. The process of liaison with these groups can itself create the focus of a local debate about carers' issues. (See Chapter 6 for more on carers' groups.)

It may be helpful to draw together some principles for policy making in this area. Listed below are some suggestions which could be added to and amended to fit local circumstances. You may find it useful to discuss this list with colleagues.

DEVELOPING POLICY

Policy statements
In developing policies on community care, national and local agencies should make it clear that they recognise and value the massive contribution made by carers. Policies must also be framed around an understanding that many carers experience difficulties in recognising themselves as carers. They should explicitly state:

- a determination to share the responsibilities of care
- a commitment to giving both carers and the people they care for opportunities and choices to develop their lives, with as few restrictions as possible.
- that service providers should always take carers' needs into account.

Organisation
- Services should be organised to support carers, as well as the people they care for.
- Services should never be reserved solely for people with no carers. It should be clearly stated that the presence of a carer, particularly a female carer, will not be used to reduce or refuse services.
- The amount and nature of services provided should be worked out in full consultation with carers as partners.
- A carers' development worker should be employed to promote the interests of carers and to educate professionals and the general public about the special

to voice their own needs.

- Employers and providers of education and leisure services should ensure that carers have full access to jobs and community facilities.

Training

- Agencies should provide training for all their workers, including professionals, care assistants and home helps, in listening to carers' needs and treating them as partners. These skills should be valued and built into career development plans. Carers should be involved in these training programmes, to provide first-hand perspectives on their needs.
- Staff should be trained to recognise the potential conflicts between carers and the people they care for. They should not try to resolve these conflicts, but should be available to mediate as necessary. They should be trained to respect the views of both parties and to try to reach agreements which value the freedom and dignity of both. This will help to create services which help to find a balance between carers and the people they care for giving both mutual involvement and individual independence.

A Carers' Worker: the Support for Informal Carers Project, Sutton

The Support for Informal Carers project was set up in 1985, with joint funding from the London Borough of Sutton Social Services Department and Merton and Sutton District Health Authority. The brief of the project's officer was to research carers' needs and the services available to support them, to disseminate information and develop support groups, and to formulate proposals for change in both policy and practice. Underpinning this was a concern to promote an understanding of carers' needs among those working in both the statutory and voluntary sectors.

A Study Day, involving over 100 professionals in health and social services and some carers as teachers and enablers was held at the outset of the project. The carers' dimension is one part of the regular induction training for new staff in the social services department and the community nursing service. Three carers' support groups have been established, two of which are now involved in the Sutton branch of the Carers' National Association. The latter also produces a monthly newsletter, distributed to nearly 300 carers and 100 professionals. A Crossroads Care Attendant Scheme, providing services to 80 families, and a voluntary sitting service, helping about 60 families in 1987, have also been set up. An information service specifically for carers now operates within the borough's Citizens Advice Bureau. Short 'carer craft' courses are being established in local health clinics. It can be seen that a key function of this project has been to alert local service providers to the needs of carers.

CREATING A FLEXIBLE AND RESPONSIVE SERVICE

2

*'We didn't know what a social worker was. I thought
a social worker was for someone who'd been in trouble.'*

**Services tailored to carers' individual circumstances, needs
and views, through discussion at the time help is planned.**

It can be organisationally difficult for some agencies to adapt to the needs of
carers. Many have traditionally organised their services around the needs of
elderly, ill or disabled people. There are problems in changing from this model
to one which is sufficiently flexible and allows enough choice to meet carers'
needs too. An overall scarcity of resources, combined with inadequate
procedures for defining individual needs, leaves many carers 'making do' with
the wrong kind of support. Some receive less help than they need; others get
services in the wrong form. A patchwork of different support services over a
local authority area may look like choice from a planner's perspective, but can
add up to little choice for the individual carer. Little comfort can be derived from
knowing that a sitting service or other help would be available a few miles away.
The offer of residential respite care to a carer who needs a regular sitter for a
couple of hours means resources poorly used.

Developing a service that is flexible and responsive to individual needs is
likely to require change in the organisation of services and change in working

**PROBLEMS IN
ORGANISATION**

relationships. The main elements of such organisation are likely to include:

- Assessments made on a multi-disciplinary basis, taking into account emotional needs as well as 'objective' factors, such as the mental condition of the person cared for or the facilities available within the home. Assessment for different services should take place as much as possible at the same time and lead to the development of a support plan in consultation with the carer and the person needing care.
- Help in pulling together the particular services carers need. This is likely to involve many differing agencies: statutory and voluntary as well as private care organisations.
- Simpler access to services. Carers should be offered direct access to services, ensuring a more immediate response to any request.
- Regular reviews which can take stock of the situation and evaluate the support being offered. Reviews should also re-examine fundamental assumptions underlying the support plan such as the capacity and willingness of the carer to continue caring.
- Continuing information to carers about the state of their 'case'. Sometimes a decision is taken to withdraw services or close the case and the carer does not know. This is unreasonable and makes day-to-day planning difficult.
- Accommodating the separate interests of the carer and the person needing care by mediating where appropriate, between conflicting interests or, if necessary, arranging for each party to have access to their own advocate. The arrangements for joint and separate advocacy developed by the Case Management Service provide a useful model (see box on page 21).

REVIEWING CURRENT PROVISION

The questions below suggest that you reflect on the kind of services in your local area and their distribution and delivery.

- How are flexibility and choice for carers and the people they care for built in to different levels of the service, for example,
  - in policy statements and decisions?
  - in the organisation and accessibility of services?
  - in the practice of individuals who offer or 'gatekeep' services?
  - in awareness of and attitudes to carers' needs?
- Think about one or two individual carers known to you.
  - how are their needs assessed and defined at present?
  - how many different people and services do they have to deal with?
  - how far are they consulted about what is offered?
  - how do they get access to services they need?

– how much choice are they offered?
– what information are they given and how often?
    You may find it helpful to discuss these questions with a colleague and to seek the views of carers.

Listed below are eight suggestions for making services more flexible and responsive to carers' needs. Most of them are organisational and policy changes which also require a change of attitude and approach.

- Identify those already in practice in your organisation or local area
- Identify any you would like to see implemented
- For any you would like to see implemented, think about:
    – how feasible this would be
    – who should be responsible for implementation
    – what you could do to start the process of implementation. Depending on the idea and your position this could mean anything from discussing the issue with colleagues and canvassing support to formulating a proposal or allocating resources.

SUGGESTIONS FOR ACTION

Personal coordinator schemes

Many innovative schemes are beginning to demonstrate the value of providing clients with a personal coordinator. He or she can give information about available options, improve access to resources and act as an advocate on a carer's behalf. This is often called a 'key worker', but as there are many varying expectations associated with this, the term 'coordinator' is preferred here. This kind of role is also advocated in the Griffiths report where the coordinator is referred to as a care manager and has considerable control over resources. The first concern of any coordinator should of course be to provide the most appropriate service to each individual carer. A personal coordinator may work in a variety of ways:

■ **As the link between the client and a particular service-giving structure,** pulling together an individual care 'package'. The structure may be a single organisation or a multi-disciplinary unit, such as a community dementia team or a community mental handicap team. The post of coordinator may be a special post or it may be shared among different members of a team, who take on coordinator responsibilities for different clients. In either case, the coordinator has a measure of direct responsibility for managing the care package. In some cases, the coordinator is a caseworker for the person needing care and will draw in other professionals and resources as appropriate. In others, the coordinator's role is to oversee the management of a case, liaising with the workers who deliver services.

- **As a broker or intermediary,** pulling together services from a variety of sources, including neighbourhood and informal networks, to develop appropriate support. The service providers retain responsibility for management and standard setting. In the case of private and informal care, this is worked out between the person giving the service and the carer. The Kent Community Care Project, in which social workers have been used as case managers in control of a budget, is a well-known example of this approach.
- **As a free agent outside the boundaries of established services.** This approach can be particularly effective where carers have little systematic contact with formal services. This can be demonstrated by the resource worker project developed by the Family Fund. Five independent social workers with specialist expertise maintained regular contact with families of children with disabilities. It was their responsibility to identify unmet needs as well as to plan and coordinate the delivery of appropriate services. An independent coordinator also has greater freedom to develop an advocacy role on behalf of carers and the people they care for, or to encourage them to do this on their own.

Improving accessibility

This may be achieved by:

- **Recognising the needs of carers in the strategic planning of services.** This is partly a matter of what is provided and partly one of where services are set up. Decisions about the siting of fixed resources such as day centres, should take into account where carers live and what transport arrangements are available to them. The differing needs of certain groups of carers, such as those from ethnic minority communities, also demand attention here. For some services, such as respite and home care services, there will be a need to recruit black and ethnic minority workers and volunteers who have a closer understanding of their needs (See Chapter 3).
- **Generating services at neighbourhood level.** This might be done by building on existing informal networks developed by carers. The Sharecare project in Stockport, for example, began with a handful of families living in one neighbourhood who offered each other an occasional break. With social services help, it now offers somewhat more formalised family-based respite care for children with disabilities with the help of a paid coordinator.

- **Developing community based services through consultation with local groups.** For example, the Nottingham Community Mental Handicap Teams have supported the efforts of several local parents' groups to create facilities for their children. These now include parent-run playschemes, a community house with short-stay respite care beds and a training house which enables young adults to develop skills for independent living.
- **Mobilising the help of neighbours** and residents is another approach. Some community care schemes have enabled carers to buy in specific services from their neighbours, using public funds.
- **Simplifying access to services.** Oldham Social Services Department, for instance, decided to eliminate field social workers' role as gatekeepers to a short-stay residential unit. Advertisements for the unit were placed in the local evening paper and carers were encouraged to make direct requests for respite care. Fears that the service would be swamped proved unfounded, but the more open approach attracted many carers who had not previously been in touch with any formal services.

DEVELOPING POLICY

It may be helpful to draw together some principles for policy making in this area. Listed below are some suggestions which could be added to and amended to fit local circumstances. You may find it useful to discuss this list with colleagues.

Policy statements

Policies for carers and the people they care for are in a state of transition and new dilemmas are being faced. Proposals to give professionals more concentrated power raise questions about their use of discretion and the rights of carers. Policy needs to balance the benefits of good overall coordination and consumer choice.

- Community care policies should promote the principles of flexibility and choice in meeting the needs of carers and the people they care for.
- A range of different forms of support should be offered: carers should be able to choose from this range the amounts and combinations of help that they need. As carers' needs change over time, these should be regularly reviewed.
- Local service providers should be urged to work in partnership with carers, providing information and helping them to obtain services.
- It should be a formal policy commitment that professionals are viewed as facilitators of services, helping carers to choose, rather than prescribers of a set amount of services.

Organisation

The expectation of organisational change contained in reports such as those of Griffiths, Wagner and the Health Service Review make it difficult to make firm proposals.

- While services remain fragmented, a link person or coordinator should be provided to carers and people needing care. This person should have an overview of the services available in the area, provided by statutory, voluntary and private agencies. He or she should consult carers to help clarify their particular needs, offering advice as appropriate. Where carers wish, the coordinator might serve as an 'advocate', representing their views and interests to other agencies. The coordinator role can be organised in several ways.
- Carers should have a continuing support plan, which is regularly reviewed, based on discussion with the carer and person needing care.
- Resources should be planned to offer carers a wide variety of services within their own local areas. These need to include services appropriate to the needs of ethnic minority carers.
- Access to services, such as day care and respite care, should be simplified.

Training

- The role of coordinator should be clearly defined and appropriate training provided. This should include a detailed understanding of the services and benefits available to carers and how to obtain them.
- Training should ensure an adequate understanding of the caring relationship and develop the capacity to look at services from a carer's point of view.

Coordination and advocacy

'Choice' a Case Management Service in Camden is an independent voluntary project which provides a direct service to people with a physical disability and their carers in the London Boroughs of Camden and Islington. Its fundamental aim is to connect the client to the services he or she needs by providing a case manager, who plans, coordinates, monitors and reviews an appropriate package of care in collaboration with the client and carer. The case manager has no direct service giving responsibilities and can therefore pursue the client's interests wholeheartedly.

The freedom to cross boundaries between agencies and sectors means that appropriate services can be obtained from any source, including private agencies and informal networks. The case manager also has the capacity to act as an advocate for clients, either negotiating on their behalf directly with service providers or pursuing their case through complaints and appeals procedures. Many clients who have fallen through the net of service provision or who are in conflict with a service providing agency have benefited from the project's advocacy role. The case management service seeks to maximise the interests of carers as well as clients, but recognises that the two parties may sometimes have quite different objectives. If there is evident conflict of interest here, which cannot be resolved through mediation by the case manager, the project will provide a second case manager to focus exclusively on the carer.

Assessment: an innovative model

One innovative model of assessment has been created within the Care for Elderly People at Home Project in Gloucester. This aims to improve the quality of support for frail elderly people living at home, through care coordinators attached to three primary health care teams for a three-year experimental period. A distinctive feature of the assessment process is a biographical interview, which explores the elderly person's life history and explores belief patterns. The way this approach is used varies with each person. By providing information about key relationships and the person's ability to cope with changing circumstances, it creates a basis for confidence and trust between the care coordinator and the client. As the project has found, a similar approach is useful in exploring the carer's perspective: it can lead to a better understanding of the carer as a person with distinctive needs and relationships beyond the caring tasks.

Coordination as case management

The Darlington Community Care Project provides a well-developed example of this approach. A joint health and social services initiative, this supports mentally alert but physically disabled elderly people who would otherwise need continuing hospital care. Paid home care assistants perform a wide range of domestic tasks and, under professional direction, provide therapy, including speech therapy exercises and physiotherapy, and support; they may also help families to claim welfare benefits. The home care assistants are linked to a range of specialised professionals who act as case coordinators, constructing care plans, chasing progress and liaising with carers.

3

THE NEEDS OF BLACK & ETHNIC MINORITY CARERS

'Asians feel much more stigma about handicap. They're not likely to bring it out into the open. Some members (of my carers' group) feel that if you're a different colour, you're backward .... They think if you're Asian you can't speak English and don't bother to speak to you. That's why many come and leave again. But I can stand on my own two feet.'

Services which reflect an awareness of differing racial, cultural and religious backgrounds and values, equally accessible to carers of every race and ethnic origin.

UNDERSTANDING THE ISSUES

Many different races, cultures and religions make up British society today. The diversity defies easy description. Some black and ethnic minority communities are composed of people with origins in one area of one country and are very close-knit. Other people within the black and ethnic minority populations do not belong to a 'community' at all. There are differing approaches to medicine and healing, different perceptions of illness, disability and old age and differing responses to the tasks of caring.

In the most economically deprived areas of the inner cities, where black and ethnic minority populations are concentrated, the number of carers receiving help from the statutory services appears to be disproportionately small. Similarly, few belong to, or participate in, the larger and more established voluntary organisations which provide support and help to carers.

Those providing services should be cautious in the assumptions which they make about the needs of black or ethnic minority carers. A common assumption among many service providers is that there is an extended family, particularly for Asian and Chinese families, which can invariably provide. This is true for some, but not for all. The immigration process may have destroyed the extended family. In addition, many aspects of life in modern Britain weaken networks or their capacity to provide sufficient support and care. Housing and employment difficulties can often separate parents and their adult children. Few houses or flats can readily accommodate more than two generations or related households.

Similarly, it should not be assumed that because people do not come forward for services such as day care or home help that these are neither needed nor wanted. The content of services and the ways in which they are provided may not reflect the diversity of carers' needs and the realities of their lives. These realities may include discrimination and racism. The growth of racial abuse, harassment and attacks in many parts of the country may create a climate in which access to services feels very limited indeed.

The spectrum of needs which black and ethnic minority carers share is no different from that of all other carers. They, too, need information, respite care, practical help, someone to talk to and so forth as explored in other chapters of this book. The issues which arise are ones concerned with securing equal access to these services and equal treatment. For some carers, however, there may be a need for some new services, taking account of diversity of language, culture and experience.

The level of unmet need is unknown. There may be some carers and their families, living in a close-knit community, who can provide their own network of support and neither want nor need help from the statutory services. There are others, however, where the experience of attempting to get services has been so painful that they would rather do without. Some of these carers are desperate. Improved access needs to be given some priority.

Creating a service that is responsive to the diverse needs of these different sections of the community is likely to require developments in the following areas.

Information-giving

Information is a problem for all carers, but black and ethnic minority carers often live in even greater isolation than others, especially where they speak little English. Some are simply not in touch with any service, but some service providers do not remember to tell carers about what is available. Ignorance may be compounded where carers have recently arrived in this country and do not expect benefits or services to be available, as they do not exist in their country of origin.

Recognition of racism

Service providers must be able to deal directly with enquiries from black and ethnic minority carers. There has been insufficient recognition of the racism which affects the everyday dealings of people who are not white. This has no place in the delivery of services to anyone including carers and the people they care for. Experience of discrimination has a long-lasting effect. People who suffer it regularly will remain sceptical about their access to services, however sensitive and encouraging the publicity material is. Patronising or dismissive attitudes on the part of professionals or 'gatekeepers' can leave an enduring sting.

Sensitivity and responsiveness

Service providers need to give attention to each family's circumstances when planning the services to be provided. For some families it will be critical to ensure that staff are themselves from black and ethnic minority communities. Greater consultation with black and ethnic minority carers may be needed as well as continual monitoring and review to ensure that services remain appropriate.

Special services

People from minority groups may feel more comfortable with services which are focussed not only on the condition of the person they care for but also on people from a similar background. Service providers may need to look at the employment of specialist workers and the establishment of special groups. For example, there is a growing number of groups throughout the country for Asian parents of children with learning difficulties.

Positive policies

Many local authorities in multi-racial areas have switched from a colourblind approach to a more positive race equality policy. Some progress is being made in recruitment and career development, so that staff are slowly beginning to reflect the communities they serve. This is not simply a matter of hiring a race advisor or social worker in a specialist capacity. There is a need for staff at all levels who can plan and deliver services effectively to carers from different backgrounds. At the policy level, this is important in making services more appropriate and accessible to black and ethnic minority carers. At the level of service delivery, it can be essential in making services more acceptable. Service providers should monitor their recruitment policies and set targets appropriately.

Many existing services are not appropriate to the needs of black and ethnic minority carers and the people they care for. This is particularly visible in the case of services for elderly people. It does not take much imagination, for example, to understand the situation of an elderly woman whose only language is Mandarin who is placed in a day centre where staff and other users speak only English. Nor is language the only – or even the most serious – problem. An elderly woman of Caribbean origin with excellent English will suffer heavily if she is placed in a day centre where she is the only non-white and likely to experience racism. There are also questions of differing needs, such as dietary requirements, bathing arrangements and hair and skin care, which are not always met by existing services.

The questions below suggest that you reflect on your awareness of the needs of people from different racial, cultural and religious backgrounds and the appropriateness of the services your organisation provides for them.
- What recognition is given to people from black and ethnic groups in:
  – policy guidelines and decisions?
  – practice guidelines?
  – monitoring and review practices?
- Thinking of a particular establishment or service you know well:
  – How easy do people from, for example, an Afro-Caribbean, Asian or Chinese background find it to approach this service?
  – What training and experience do workers in this service have in dealing with clients from an Afro-Caribbean, Asian or Chinese background, or from any other black or ethnic minority community?
  – What proportion of clients using this service are from black and ethnic minority groups? Does this reflect their proportion in the population of the area?

You may find it helpful to discuss these questions with a colleague and to seek the views of carers from black and ethnic minority groups.

Listed below are seventeen suggestions for developing a service that is accessible and responsive to carers of every race and ethnic origin. Some concern changes in attitude and practice, some suggest particular projects, some are about shifts in policy that could affect the whole service.

- Identify those already in practice in your organisation or local area
- Identify any you would like to see implemented
- For any you would like to see implemented think about:
  - how feasible this would be
  - who should be responsible for implementation
  - what you could do to start the process of implementation. Depending on the idea and your position this could mean anything from discussing the issue with colleagues and canvassing support through to formulating a proposal or allocating resources.

■ **Consultation with black and ethnic minority carers.** Service providers need to talk to representatives of carers from the different communities to find out their needs and the adjustments to services they consider desirable. This means detailed and continuing discussion. A consultative meeting involving senior officers from health and social services is not enough. Consultation should be carried out in self-help groups, voluntary organisations, local community centres, churches, mosques and temples. As black and ethnic minority carers are not a homogenous group and as some groups are much more articulate and organised than others, consultation may require a number of different strategies. (See Chapter 10).

■ **Employing a specialist social worker or outreach worker** familiar with a particular community and able to communicate with its members. This person might help groups to get started and provide assistance in fund-raising and other aspects of group maintenance. The Social Services Department in the London Borough of Haringey, for example, employs a community worker who has helped to develop a support group for Afro-Caribbean parents of young mentally ill people. This role can also be played by the voluntary sector. SCEMSC (the Standing Conference on Ethnic Minority Senior Citizens) provides help to local groups in London, in securing funding and meeting other needs.

■ **Encouraging specialist self-help groups.** Voluntary organisations for black and ethnic minority people are often able to provide services which are especially responsive to their needs. This may be because they are small and because they have a highly participative approach. The Pepperpot Club in Kensington is one example, providing a day centre for elderly Afro-Caribbean people, with recreation, companionship, support and advice. This offers valuable respite for carers as they know the person they care for will feel at home there.

■ **Monitoring and evaluating services** for their appropriateness. The issue of take-up deserves particular attention, so as to identify potential groups which are not getting the services they need. Monitoring should be built into service planning in all areas, but may be particularly important where there is a large black and ethnic population.

■ **Providing translation** for carers who do not speak or read English. Translations need to be available in appropriate languages and in an understandable form. Information on how to get services and how to complain should be given particular attention. Complex legal jargon about benefits and procedures, or difficult medical terminology, often does not translate well. Translations should be developed in consultation with black and ethnic minority groups. The existence of such information needs to be well publicised.

■ **Newsletters** can be useful in disseminating information to ethnic minority carers. For example, Contact a Family in Southall produces a newsletter for parents in four Asian languages, providing carers with a great deal of valuable information.

■ **Alternatives to the written word** need to be explored. Some ethnic minority carers have received only a limited education or are illiterate in their own language. The use of ethnic minority community radio in some cities can offer direct contact with housebound carers whose understanding of English is limited. Audio cassette tapes, which can be played in carers' own homes, are another way of producing information. These should be well publicised.

■ **Video films** targeted at specific groups, can explain a range of services to carers, for example chiropody or continence services. Some social services departments are making progress in this area and there are several informative videos aimed at the needs of minority communities. Scope, a project for Asian elders in Leicester and Leicester Council for Voluntary Service have jointly developed a video for carers. Videos should be well publicised and made available for viewing in community centres, day centres and residential homes.

■ **Home visits** bringing information, may be needed by some carers. These could be done by people who are working with carers or by someone who speaks their language and is likely to have some understanding of their circumstances.

■ **Use of schools.** Another route for some families is through written material given to children to bring home from school. This may give it added importance and, even when in English, can be read either by someone else in the family or by a neighbour or friend.

■ **Presentation of information**. Posters and other illustrative material should be inclusive of all races and backgrounds, for example using photographs of Asian, Afro-Caribbean and Chinese people. In addition, publicity material might explicitly encourage black and ethnic minority carers, and the people they care for, to take up services.

■ **Interpreters** can be instrumental in opening up services to those whose command of English is limited. They need not only linguistic skills but also an understanding of the policies and practices of the services. They should be regularly employed and trained in the needs of carers and the people they care for. It is important that they are called in to help when a carer needs help and not just when a professional finds it difficult to communicate. Ad hoc interpreting can result in a great deal of misunderstanding.

■ **Employing staff from black and ethnic minority communities.** Some carers may not feel able to accept help from a care attendant or home help who does not understand the important aspects of their culture. Employing workers from black and ethnic minority communities should lead to a more sensitive and responsive service.

■ **Career development for black and ethnic minority workers.** Black and ethnic minority staff should be assured of access to training and promotion.

■ **Reviewing grant-giving policies.** More established voluntary organisations should be urged to ensure that their services are accessible to people from all communities. Many of these have few black or ethnic minority members. Some are aware of this and are attempting to rectify it, but it is also important to ensure that black and ethnic minority groups are able to get financial help. Grants made to smaller groups, especially those providing services such as meals-on-wheels or day care, are often more effective in reaching these communities. Help to the growing number of black and ethnic minority self-help initiatives may also serve to bring their members' attention to services.

■ **Establishing posts concerned with equal opportunity,** focussing on employment issues, service delivery or both. Most of those that currently exist are in local authorities, but some health authorities are beginning to have such posts. These may be helpful with respect to carers' issues. Haringey Health Authority, for instance, employs an officer whose brief includes attention to service delivery for black and ethnic minority groups.

■ **Staff training** has an important part to play in an overall programme of change. It is important that service planners review their training regularly to ensure that it is appropriate for a multi-racial society.

It may be helpful to draw together some principles for policy making in this area. Listed below are some suggestions which could be added to and amended to fit local circumstances. You may find it useful to discuss these ideas with colleagues.

DEVELOPING POLICY

Policy statements

All policy statements should contain the clear direction that services to carers and the people they care for should never discriminate on grounds of race, culture or religion.

- Policies should extend the range of choices available to black and ethnic minority carers, both by making existing services more accessible and by developing new services.
- There should be genuine consultation with black and ethnic minority carers.
- Provision should be reviewed to ensure that services do not deter black and ethnic minority carers and the people they care for, either because of direct or indirect racism or because of inappropriate arrangements, such as routines and diet.
- Policies should seek to ensure that black and ethnic minority staff are employed at all levels, both to devise suitable provision and to provide suitable understanding of carers' needs when working directly with them. Employment policies should be reviewed to ensure that there are equal opportunities for advancement.

Organisation

- Services should be developed which are appropriate to the needs of black and ethnic minority carers. Written information about services should be translated. Other means of providing information, such as audio cassettes and videos in different languages, should be used.
- Skilled interpreters should be used.
- Financial help and other support should be provided to enable black and ethnic minority carers to set up their own organisations and to strengthen informal networks. Support workers should come from differing racial, ethnic and religious backgrounds.
- Grants to voluntary organisations should be reviewed to ensure they are available to black and ethnic minority groups.
- Staff in all agencies and at all levels should reflect the multi-racial community, with full opportunities for career development. Equal opportunity policies should be monitored and evaluated.

Training

- All staff should be trained to work effectively in a multi-racial and multi-cultural society.
- Black and ethnic minority staff should be given access to training and promotion. Interpreters should be trained to be familiar with issues concerning carers and caring and all staff should be trained to work with interpreters.

Services for ethnic minority carers: the ICAN Asian Family Support Centre, Smethwick

The Asian Family Support Centre was set up by ICAN (Invalid Children's Aid Nationwide) in June 1986, following research on the problems faced by Asian families with children with disabilities. All staff speak two or three Asian languages. Families are visited once a week and offered practical help and emotional support. Liaison workers can give advice about welfare benefits, housing, education and social and medical problems. They may also accompany the health visitor on a routine visit to parents' homes and they will arrange transport and accompany families to hospitals,

GPs' surgeries or the DHSS office. A mothers' support group exists and mothers are encouraged to share their problems in an atmosphere of trust and understanding.

The Centre is staffed by an organiser (funded under Opportunities for Volunteering), a team leader, a sessional social worker, (funded by DHSS Caring for Carers project in Sandwell) and a team of six part-time liaison workers (funded by the MSC). The number of families involved has grown from an initial 23 to 70.

OPPORTUNITIES FOR A BREAK

'You can't make any plans. We haven't been out together for months and it looks like going on for years.'

Opportunities for a break, both for short spells (an afternoon) and for longer periods (a week or more), to relax and have time for themselves.

RESPITE CARE

Carers need some time to themselves. Caring for a confused elderly person, someone who has had a stroke or a child with severe learning difficulties can be a 24 hour job, 7 days a week, 52 weeks a year. Carers do not have their hours of work controlled to protect their health. They tend to become both physically and emotionally exhaused. This brings in its wake stress, despair and family breakdown. Like everyone else, carers need time to do what they want – to be by themselves as well as to maintain friendships. In the absence of a break, they can lose these ties. Sometimes, just the knowledge that a break is available can make a real difference to a carers' sense of support.

Respite care covers all the different ways in which carers can get some time off. It can be provided inside the home and outside it, for both short and longer periods and may be planned or unplanned. Planned respite care allows carers to think ahead, to arrange a trip out for the day, to have a holiday or maintain a job. Unplanned respite care is needed in a crisis, for example, if the carer has 'flu or has to go into hospital. Both are important. Carers should be able to plan ahead, with the knowledge that respite will be available on a regular basis. When they reach breaking point or simply become ill, they need help quickly. An effective respite service will include the elements described below.

A range of options

Like everyone else, carers have differing needs for work or relaxation. Some need regular help to enable them to maintain a job. Some may want the occasional morning or afternoon off – to go to church, or a football match or to do some shopping. Others may prefer an evening off, to go out with friends or to attend an evening class. Still others may feel their real need is for a full week or fortnight off once a year. Some may want to have the person cared for taken out so they can have the house to themselves. Carers should be able to choose the kind of care that most suits their own needs and domestic arrangements. Respite care should not be offered on a take-it or leave-it basis.

Understanding difficulties

Those providing services must recognise that carers may have difficulties using respite care. A lack of enthusiasm does not mean that carers do not need a break. Carers may find it difficult to trust other people with the care of the person they look after and may need encouragement to use respite care. Often those in greatest need are those least able to make the decision. There is a great deal of guilt about taking a break, even for a short period. This may be compounded where the person being cared for is resistant to the idea. Conflicts between the carer and the person needing care need sensitive handling. Workers can too easily respond to the needs of the person needing care and tell the carer 'we can't force her to go'. There may be a need for someone to mediate here, to help the person needing care to appreciate the need for a break and to encourage the carer to make use of their services on a short-term basis initially. Someone should take the responsibility for discussing the issue, exploring the possible need for a break and pointing out that it may also be best for the person cared for. They should give carers time to air their doubts and anxieties. The Alzheimers Disease Society South Cleveland Project, which runs six day centres, spends some time talking to carers to encourage them to use their services.

A personal service

All respite services need to be based on trusting personal relationships. These can take time to get established and do not always develop easily. Once a relationship has been struck, sitter services can be particularly effective in developing a high degree of trust and flexibility. Carers can be allocated a set number of days per year to call on when required, by direct arrangement. The

Brent Triangle scheme offers support to carers of elderly mentally infirm people through paid and trained care attendants who provide respite care in carers' own homes in regular weekly sessions. The amount of support provided is negotiated between a coordinator from the scheme and the carer and is based on the carer's perceived need for support and relief.

Respect for privacy and individuality

Any scheme providing respite in the home must remember that a home is a private place. Having anyone come in – even to help – can seem an intrusion. This will be even greater where there is any suggestion that the care provided by the outsider is in some way better. Carers and the people they care for need reassurance that the sitter will carry out tasks in the same way as the carer. Of course, those providing help may have hints about how to ease the carer's job, but great sensitivity will be needed in offering them. It should also be remembered that some carers may feel ashamed about the state of their house, or the condition of the person cared for. Considerable sensitivity will be needed here.

Knowledge and training

All those who work with carers – GPs, social workers, home helps, staff of special schools – need to make themselves fully familiar with the range of local respite services. They are in a key position to tell carers about them and encourage carers on the brink of crisis to make a decision to use them.

There is a clear need for training for any person providing care in the home. Families need to feel that the person doing the job knows something about the particular illness or condition of the person needing care. Willing amateurs are not likely to win many friends. In addition, each family has its own way of doing things and sitters should be open to learning from them. Some carers are more expert on the condition than the professionals with whom they come into contact. They are certainly more expert with regard to the person they care for. Some organisations, including the Crossroads Care Attendant Scheme, include training by the carer in their programme.

The questions below suggest that you reflect on the provision of respite care in your area and its quality and effectiveness.

REVIEWING CURRENT PROVISION

- What acknowledgement of carers' needs for a break exists in:
  - policy statements about carers and the people they care for
  - admissions policies of residential establishments

        – the practices of different establishments and services
        – in-service training
- Think about one or two individual carers known to you
        – what needs for a break do they have?
        – what services can be provided to meet these needs?
        – how satisfactory do they find these services?
        – what reservations might they have about using these services?
        – how easy is it for the carers themselves to gain access to each of these services?

You may find it helpful to discuss these questions with a colleague and to seek the views of carers as these may differ from those of workers.

SUGGESTIONS FOR ACTION Listed below are eleven suggestions for action that could help to develop opportunities for carers to take a break. They range from changes in attitude and practice on the part of those running the service to changes in organisation and systems and the development of new services.

- Identify those already in practice in your organisation or local area
- Identify any you would like to see implemented
- For any you would like to see implemented, think about:
        – how feasible this would be
        – who should be responsible for implementation
        – what you could do to start the process of implementation. Depending on the idea and your position this could mean anything from discussing the issue with colleagues and canvassing support to formulating a proposal or allocating resources.

■ **Organising short stay places.** Short term care should be carefully planned around the needs of the person being cared for and the carer. Homes for long stay residents and hospitals providing acute care are not always the best places as short term care may be viewed as an 'incidental' activity. Short term care might be provided either in a completely separate facility or with another family. It may be important for the person being cared for to maintain links with the local community (friends, library, church, for example) even when receiving respite care.

■ **Family care schemes** allow the person needing care to be looked after by another family for a weekend, a week or even longer. Carers are sometimes anxious about such arrangements, doubting whether an ordinary family can look after the person needing care as well as they do, but they can work very well.

They provide the person needing care with a break in a non-institutional setting, where his or her particular needs can be addressed. They also offer the chance to develop new relationships.

Great care must be taken in the selection of families for such schemes. They need to be given both support and training for the job. Arrangements need to be made to cope when relationships break down. The person being fostered, whether a child or elderly person, needs to be well prepared for the break. Many social services departments have such family placement arrangements. Leeds is one long-standing example. In some schemes, families are paid only a small amount – not much more than expenses: the Lothian Share the Care project is an example here.

■ **Day care** can also be seen as a kind of respite service and should try to take carers' needs into account making provision flexible enough to fit in with carers' needs. All arrangements should seek to ensure that they are accessible to black and ethnic minority carers and provide services appropriate to their particular needs, for instance with respect to diet.

- Day centres with flexible arrangements can, for example, enable working carers to retain their jobs, provide emergency facilities for a few hours in the evening or overnight or offer care at weekends. The Hillside Centre, in Plympton, Devon provides day care for elderly mentally infirm people as well as a residential unit. It has staff on the premises day and night, so that carers can use it as and when they need.
- Playgroups open to very young children with disability provide badly needed respite for parents.
- Day hospitals providing treatment and other help are often highly valued by carers for the break they provide.

■ **Befriending schemes** are normally set up with the joint intention of providing stimulation and fun for the person cared for, while offering a break to the carer. They are particularly common for people with learning difficulties. Such schemes can prove highly successful. They provide opportunities to pursue new activities and an avenue to company and emotional support. Problems can arise with the dual function of such schemes and it is important to be alert to this. There are many befriending schemes around the country, for example, the Sharing Care project in Leeds has organised 60 links between befrienders and people with learning difficulties.

■ **Holidays** for people needing care are another way of providing a respite for carers. Where the carer does not want a full separation, a family holiday with a companion who can relieve the carer of some caring tasks is an imaginative version of respite care.

■ **Sitting services** provide carers some hours to themselves usually during the day or evening. Night sitting services are invaluable to carers who are otherwise denied a proper night's sleep. The sitters may be paid or unpaid. Some families prefer the sitter to be paid, mainly because they feel they have more control. A coordinator to meet and match families and sitters is essential. There are many examples of sitting services. The Sitter Service of the Scottish Council for Single Parents provides sitters for short periods. In Safe Hands, run by Age Concern in York, provides paid sitters who will stay for any period, from a few hours or days to a period of up to a week.

■ **Direct access.** Carers need to feel that they can use respite care without creating a fuss. In the case of formal services, use of respite care will be made easier through direct access to the service. This means the carer has no need to go through a social worker or other person with a gatekeeping function. The fact that direct applications can be made should be well advertised. The staff involved may need special training to cope with carers' requests and concerns.

■ **Informal schemes.** With informal arrangements, carers may find it helpful to have a set number of hours each week which can be altered in an emergency. Some authorities provide carers with vouchers to use as they need. Schemes should be small-scale and locally organised. Procedures and paperwork should be pared to the minimum. Carers will also feel less inhibited about asking for a break if they know they will not have to explain everything to a stranger unfamiliar with their domestic circumstances and routine.

■ **Lump sum schemes.** Even greater accessibility and flexibility can be achieved if carers are provided with a lump sum to spend how they like. The London Borough of Sutton, which set up such an arrangement, found that some carers bought in care from a private agency while others arranged for a holiday for the person needing care. Of course, in some circumstances, it may not be possible to buy in appropriate services.

■ **Publicity.** Carers need to know that respite care is available and in what forms. Arrangements need to be well publicised. Services should be advertised directly in local newspapers, including the ethnic minority press. Articles describing the services provided will help carers know what they are about. A Carers' Centre could be very useful here, providing information on all local respite services. (See Chapter 7).

■ **Consultation** at the planning stage will ensure that respite services reflect carers' interests. Carers can also be involved later, for example represented on the management or steering committee. The FACE/STOP schemes in Newcastle, which provide family care for children and adults with learning difficulties involved parents in this way.

It may be helpful to draw together some principles for policy making in this area. Listed below are some suggestions which could be added to and amended to fit local circumstances. You may find it useful to discuss these ideas with colleagues.

POLICY DEVELOPMENT

Policy statements

Policy statements should recognise explicitly that provision of good quality respite services is fundamental to the mental and physical health of carers and to the long term success of community care.

- As individual circumstances differ, it should be policy to provide a range of services, both short and long term, inside the home and outside. These should be readily accessible and sufficiently flexible to meet carers' needs.
- It should be policy to consult carers about the adequacy, range, quality and accessibility of the respite care services provided.

Organisation

- More respite care should be provided, both outside and inside the home. This should be available to carers both in a planned way and in a crisis.
- Statutory authorities should work closely with voluntary agencies to provide choice in the services available. The coordinator should be very familiar with existing provision.
- Carers and the people they care for should be encouraged to choose the amount and kind of respite services they need. Experience shows that services are not necessarily overwhelmed with demands.
- Service providers should be able to mediate between carers and the people they care for, where conflict arises between them about the use of respite care.
- Carers should have direct access to respite care services wherever possible and facilities should be approachable and well publicised. Where there is no direct access, carers should not have to be separately assessed for use of respite care.

Training

- Staff who provide respite care should be trained:
  − to understand the medical conditions and care needs of the people for whom they are providing care and how to manage them
  − to listen and respond to the individual needs of carers and the people they care for
  − to liaise with carers about direct access arrangements. Interpreters and translations should be available.
- All staff who work with carers should be given information about the range of respite care services available. They should tell carers about these services and encourage them to make use of them.

Respite Care for Carers of Elderly Mentally Infirm People: the Family Support Unit, Middlesbrough

The Family Support Unit, Eastbourne Lodge, Middlesbrough, was set up in 1984 to help carers by providing a regular pattern of short-term respite care for elderly mentally infirm people. It is small in the number (35) catered for, but offers great flexibility. Eastbourne Lodge is a family sized house in a residential area. The Unit provides respite care for up to five people at a time, plus day care or evening care for ten people. Carers are offered residential care on rotation every five or six weeks. This can also sometimes be provided at short notice. Day care is provided two or three times a week, with help also offered in the evenings. The Unit has 18 staff, some part-time. The project is jointly funded by the South Tees District Health Authority and Cleveland County Council.

In addition to the respite services provided, the co-ordinator offers information, advice and support to carers and regular carer support group meetings. Regular personal and telephone contact is maintained with carers. A community psychiatric nurse is attached to the unit and makes home visits once a fortnight to carers who use the centre. She can provide some counselling to carers and liaise with local service providers as appropriate. She may also offer advice on the management of the confused person, keeping an eye on his or her physical and mental condition and medication.

THE PROVISION OF PRACTICAL HELP

*'When I got the Glide About chair, my life was transformed.
I didn't have to lift him from the bed and carry him to the chair
in the other room. I just wish I had known about it earlier.'*

**Practical help to lighten the tasks of caring, including
domestic help, home adaptations, incontinence services and
help with transport.**

Carers need help in the home to enable them to care as best they can. Caring
can be a great physical strain and it can also take a lot of time. The hours required
to get a demented and frail person washed, dressed and fed can cut deeply into
the time available to do other household chores, which may themselves require
extra time. Living with an incontinent person, for instance, means that washing
has to be done every day. For many carers, there is also a need for help with
transport. Without it, it may be impossible to take the person they care for out at
all.

A comprehensive service of practical help would provide assistance with
domestic and caring tasks, with aids and equipment, and with transport. It would
also offer up to date information about what is available.

TYPES OF ASSISTANCE

Aids and appliances

Carers' workloads can be eased by many aids and appliances.

To save time and labour, many need help with washing: a washing machine if they can manage at home or an incontinence laundry service if they cannot.

A telephone is also vital. Where carers are housebound, this can provide a lifeline to the outside world. It enables them to organise their lives, ask for assistance from neighbours or friends or get help in an emergency.

An enormous range of aids and equipment is available to increase the independence of people needing care. Walking frames, hoists and rails, for example, can improve mobility. Dressing sticks, raised toilet seats, bath boards, and feeding cups help both the person cared for and the carer get through the basic tasks of living with as little fuss, discomfort and strain as possible. Special clothing with velcro tape rather than buttons makes it quicker and easier to dress a disabled person.

At best these aids improve the well being and independence of the person cared for. At the very least, they release valuable time and reduce physical strain on the carer. Aids should not be pressed on carers if they do not want them, of course. Some resent their home being turned into a hospital. They need advice about alternative ways of coping with a problem, for instance replacing carpets with linoleum. Carers need to be able to choose those things that would be most useful for them.

An extra pair of hands

For many carers labour saving gadgetry is no substitute for an extra pair of hands. This may be to help with general housework, to provide help with the tasks of caring or to do other supplementary jobs, such as helping with other children or mowing the lawn. Some carers need substantial help, to enable them to keep a job or because they are unable to undertake the necessary work unaided. Some need only small amounts of help – at certain periods of the day or for a few hours a week. What is needed is imagination and flexibility in the help provided. Services need to match carers' needs and the rhythm of a carer's day.

Transport

Transport can be a real problem when carers need to take the person they care for out somewhere – to the hospital or clinic or to visit someone. Public transport is often unsuitable. The person needing care may find it difficult to get on and off a bus or train and maybe unable to stand for long periods. Even carers who can drive may be unable to do so without help if the person they care for is likely to disturb their concentration. Transport provided by social services departments is not always dependable.

Public transport could be made more accessible by some simple changes. Steps need to be lowered, hand rails positioned more appropriately and all bus stops equipped with seating and shelter. The new Docklands Light Railway has made a great effort to be accessible to disabled people and demonstrates what can be achieved when designers take them into account.

The need for information

Although there is a lot of impressive equipment available many carers do not know about it. Items in the field of feeding, clothing and continence are rarely advertised in the same way as health food products or vitamin pills. Nor are they regularly displayed, even by large dispensing chemists. Women who have had children may remember the feeding and toilet equipment used to care for a baby, but others may not be aware of simple things like a feeding cup designed for an older child or an adult. It is hard to ask for something when you do not know that it exists.

Many carers may also be unaware of who can help with transport, how to obtain grants for adaptations or how to deal with some of the more difficult or unpleasant tasks of caring. Information about all these practical things needs to be more widely available.

The questions below suggest that you reflect on the practical help for carers currently provided in your area by statutory and voluntary organisations.

REVIEWING CURRENT PROVISION

- Which organisations and establishments make provision in each of the four areas described above?
  - aids and appliances?
  - domestic help?
  - transport?
  - information?
- What principles or assumptions underlie provision? For instance, is it assumed that carers need more or less help than people living alone? Are certain categories of people more likely to get help than others? Do different sectors and organisations provide services on different principles?
- Thinking about one or two individual carers known to you
  - what needs for practical help do these people have?
  - how effectively are they met at present?
  - what prevents more effective provision being made? Attitudes? Policy? Resources? Lack of training? Lack of information?

You may find it helpful to discuss these questions with a colleague and to seek the views of carers as those may differ from those of workers.

SUGGESTIONS FOR ACTION   Listed below are sixteen suggestions for action that could improve the practical help offered to carers. They range from suggestions about the type of service that should be offered, through the provision of information about what is available and the way the service is offered.

- Identify those already in practice in your organisation or local area
- Identify any you would like to see implemented
- For any you would like to see implemented think about:
  - how feasible this would be
  - who should be responsible for implementation
  - what you could do to start the process of implementation. Depending on the idea and your position, this could mean anything from discussing the issue with colleagues and canvassing support to formulating a proposal or allocating resources.

■ **Make yourself familiar** with the range of aids available and how to get them by obtaining up to date catalogues.

■ **Ask local pharmacists** to exhibit catalogues and information describing how to get the items listed. There are examples of good practice here. Boots has produced a new range of aids for caring, as well as a catalogue, and is training staff to understand how to use them. In some areas the aids are particularly well displayed. Boots in Cambridge provides free catalogues and has a good display of many basic items.

■ **Encourage GPs' surgeries** to have information about aids to daily living in their waiting rooms. They are likely to be in regular contact with elderly and disabled patients. The local Family Practitioner Committee should be approached to gain cooperation here. Some will send out leaflets and posters to all GPs in their area.

■ **Make information available** to carers about all practical help. This is likely to include information about transport schemes (Motability, the exemption from vehicle excise duty and the orange badge scheme for disabled drivers, for example), aids and appliances, eligibility for services, grants and procedures for adaptations to the home.

■ **Explore a range of means,** from mobile exhibitions to the use of local radio (see chapter 7) for making information available. This is particularly crucial as occupational therapists are commonly in short supply.

■ **Review procedures.** Local authorities should review their procedures for getting aids. Delays here are particularly cruel. A wait of just three or four weeks may seem reasonable in organisational terms, for instance, but it is too long when caring for someone who is terminally ill. Some items might be made available for borrowing. One self-help group, for instance, keeps a 'sheet bank' for carers who do not want to buy new sheets when they have a short-term problem because of incontinence.

■ **Help carers pursue adaptations to the home.** Some heavy equipment needed by seriously immobile people may require adaptations to the home such as the construction of a bathroom downstairs. Organising such work can be very slow. For owner-occupiers, planning permission may be required and, while grants are available from the Department of the Environment, these take time to secure. Those working with carers might pursue the claim on the carer's behalf. Council tenants should be encouraged to involve their estate manager in any work undertaken. Because this work crosses departmental boundaries, local authorities should also set up an adaptations team, including people from the housing and social services departments.

■ **Provide more advice** about caring. Some of the more unpleasant tasks – for the person needing care as well as the carer – might be avoided with good advice. Advice about incontinence, for instance, should be more widely available, to help carers and reduce pressure on continence advisers.

■ **Review policy on the provision of home helps.** Home helps are often only provided to people who are coping on their own. Authorities with such a policy should think again. Carers do need help. Some authorities provide help only to male carers. This is not only unfair to women carers but it is unlawful discrimination.

■ **Provide home care assistants** who can offer more intensive help and help with more personal tasks. Again, these are sometimes available only where there is no care. They need to be available to carers too. There is a growing number of authorities with this service. One example is the social services department in the London Borough of Hounslow. Its personal care scheme provides help to elderly or disabled people, including relief to carers. Services are tailored to meet carers' needs, including help in the early morning and evening. The Home Aide service in Avon provides assistants in some cases for 24 hours a day for up to two weeks.

■ **Provide training for home care assistants.** This should include training in the skills of working with carers. The most important aspect of such help is that it should not be intrusive. In some areas, assistants will need to be from ethnic minority backgrounds, able to communicate both with the carer and the person cared for and having some understanding of differing cultural traditions.

■ **Introduce paid neighbour schemes.** Here a coordinator discusses what help is needed with the carer and then advertises locally for a paid helper. The payment involved can be small. Carers often feel payment gives greater reliability and more chance for them to supervise. In some areas, the volunteer may already be known to the carer.

■ **Provide information about private home care schemes** which offer a high standard of care. These provide many similar services to a home care assistant but must be paid for. Care Alternatives in Wimbledon is one example. This introduces care attendants to carers. They are then paid directly by the carer. The agency also provides training where appropriate. Some of the care attendants used are trained nurses.

■ **Provide out-of-hours emergency help.** Many carers face terrible dilemmas if the person cared for falls out of bed at night. A contact point should be provided and publicised to carers.

■ **Develop a closer liaison between transport services and their users** both at the point of planning and at the point of use. Although heavy traffic can make it difficult to provide precise schedules, a rough timetable is helpful. People should be told if there is a cancellation.

■ **Provide a flexible, voluntary door-to-door transport scheme,** like Dial-a-Ride or Taxicard for disabled people in London. In Plymouth, there is a community transport scheme for elderly disabled people which uses volunteer drivers. Its personal service is as flexible as a taxi but as cheap as a bus. The Vale of Evesham Volunteer Centre runs a similar car scheme, catering for some wheelchair users directly. It also works closely with a local minibus association which can provide a minibus with a hoist when required.

■ **Use volunteers to provide transport.** Volunteers who can drive could help get the person needing care to hospital when necessary or, on a more regular basis, to the local day centre. Even volunteers who could serve as an extra passenger to help with the person needing care could be a great help to some families.

DEVELOPING POLICY   It may be helpful to draw together some principles for policy making in this area. Listed below are some suggestions which could be added to and amended to fit local circumstances. You may find it helpful to discuss these ideas with colleagues.

Policy statements

Policy statements should acknowledge that caring commonly involves heavy physical work and 24-hour attention and that carers' mental and physical health are often at risk.

- Policies should be devised to meet carers' needs for a range of practical help at home, including equipment to help with domestic tasks and to provide the person needing care with more independence.
- Carers' needs for help with transport should be recognised.
- Help with personal care tasks should be provided for carers, women as well as men. Those providing such help should be able to carry out the tasks carers want and at the times carers want. They should be willing to work closely with individual carers to ensure that they provide help appropriately. Carers should be consulted about the range of practical help provided, including its amount, kind and suitability.

Organisation

- The organisation of services should be examined to ensure they are available to carers, not only to people living on their own.
- Women carers should be encouraged to make use of all help available.
- Carers should not have to be separately assessed to gain access to practical help.
- New home care assistance services should be provided to carry out more personal tasks and on a more extended basis. This may be either as an adaptation of a home help service or in addition to it. Statutory authorities may seek to give financial support to voluntary organisations providing such services, for instance those with care attendant schemes.
- Statutory authorities may also provide coordinators with a budget to buy in services for carers, to supplement statutory provision. This may be through paid neighbours and other local people as well as private care organisations.

Training

- All workers providing home care should be trained:
    - to work closely with individual carers
    - to provide care suitable to the needs of the individual person cared for
    - to provide information about the range of aids available to carers
- Carers should be involved in the training process, with opportunities for black and ethnic minority carers to explain their needs.

Providing help in the home: the Community Care Scheme, Dover, Kent

The Community Care Scheme, based on the original Thanet community care project, uses volunteers on a contractual basis to help elderly people remain in their own homes (normally until the cost rises above two-thirds of a residential placement). Some, but not all, of the elderly people have carers. The scheme is joint funded and includes an organiser and a clerical assistant.

Referrals are made via the principal social worker. Use is made of existing resources like home help, day care, meals-on-wheels and district nurses. In addition, paid helpers are brought in where necessary. These provide support for carers through help with bathing, dressing, some night sitting, day care in the carer's home and bereavement support. The organiser makes an assessment of the help needed and agrees this assessment with both the carer (where there is one) and the person needing care. He then searches for the right person to help, through contact in the voluntary sector and local churches. They are paid according to the tasks performed, rather than on an hourly basis: some prefer to pass on the fee directly to the voluntary agency. Over a 12-month period, over 50 people have been helped.

Home care assistants

This kind of help was pioneered by the voluntary sector — most notably by the Crossroads Care Attendant Scheme, but there are also other less well-known schemes. The Birmingham Multi-Handicap Group runs a parent support scheme, giving parents routine help at busy times. Care assistants help with the tasks of washing, feeding and dressing first thing in the morning and then return to do the same at night. The Options Family Support Service in Cardiff runs a service for families who have children or young people with a learning difficulty. Parents identify a task that would be useful to them and stimulating for the child. Such tasks have so far included sitting in, introducing children or young people to local community facilities and short holiday breaks.

CARERS' EMOTIONAL NEEDS

'I felt so alone — then I was told about the carers' group. I had quite a job to find it, but I'm glad I persevered. It's somewhere to come once a month. I meet people in the same boat, who know what it's like.'

Someone to talk to about their own emotional needs, at the outset of caring, while they are caring and when the caring task is over.

Perhaps carers' simplest need is for someone to talk to. They need someone who understands what it means to be a carer and who can allow them to explore their complex feelings in an atmosphere of safety and trust. Such help is needed at the outset and throughout the time of caring. It may also be important when the responsibilities of caring are over. Caring can become such a large part of life that its absence may create a considerable void. There may be feelings of guilt and loss which need to be faced. Some carers may also need support to rebuild their lives.

SOMEONE TO TALK TO

Many carers do not have anyone they can turn to. They contain their anxieties and frustrations, often at the cost of their own well-being. This is a particular problem for people caring on their own, for whom the emotional strains of caring may be exacerbated by constant fatigue. Having someone to talk to will not relieve the overload or sense of being trapped, but it may make a carer's day-to-day life somewhat easier to face.

Carers' need for someone to talk to often goes unrecognised. Family and friends, feeling uncomfortable about the carer's situation, may keep their distance. Carers, in turn, may be embarrassed about burdening others with their feelings. Professional workers who come into the home tend to focus on the person needing care, seeing the carer as just another resource in the background. Some carers unwittingly go along with this approach. They not only feel that the doctor or social worker is too busy to listen to their needs but see asking for support as a sign of failure.

A service which was able to meet carers' emotional needs would combine some of the following elements.

Responsibilities of workers

All those who come into contact with carers, whether general practitioners, community nurses, home helps, volunteer sitters or others, should be attuned to carers' need to talk. There is a need to make time for this, perhaps setting aside a regular period. This is not a matter of skilled counselling. Most carers simply need someone who will listen to their problems, from the humdrum problems of day-to-day living to the bigger, more worrying, crises. Where carers are going through a crisis, urgent practical help may be required, for instance for respite care. Those working with carers should ensure that they know who to call for help. Good links between services are particularly important here.

Counselling

Some carers need more specialised counselling. This may be needed at a time of particular crisis, such as when a condition is first diagnosed or when the person they have cared for dies. It may also be needed to explore long-term changes, such as altered family and sexual relationships or the loss of mental faculties. It is important that carers are referred on to more specialised sources of help. Those in touch with carers should seek to improve access to these, through both general information and individual guidance. Some attention may need to be paid to the differing needs of carers from ethnic minority groups due to differing backgrounds and values.

Talking to other carers

Carers also need to talk to others in the same situation. Carers' groups can provide a lifeline, offering opportunities to discuss problems and feelings in the company of people who understand because they share the experience of caring. A group can enhance self-esteem and provide moral support. It can provide a particularly safe setting for exploring emotionally charged topics and feelings, such as when to stop caring. In addition, it can provide opportunities for pressing for more or better services.

There are many kinds of carers' groups. Some are open to all carers. Others focus on carers of people with one kind of disability or a specific illness. Carers should be encouraged to seek out the one in which they would feel most at home.

In some circumstances, black and ethnic minority carers may feel more comfortable with others of the same race or background. There are growing numbers of support groups composed solely or primarily of black or ethnic minority members and it will be important to tell carers about them. Particular help should also be given with their formation. On the other hand, it should not be automatically assumed that all black or ethnic minority carers seek their own groups. Some may prefer to join existing groups open to everyone. (See Chapter 3.)

Carers' groups need to be fostered and supported. Professional workers are often uncertain about the role they should take with a self-help group. They should be willing to initiate a group or to provide continuing back-up. Indeed, support to groups should become a mainstream activity, supported and resourced at management level.

Many carers do not like groups. Some would welcome the opportunity to talk to other carers on a one-to-one basis. Professional workers should ask carers if they would like to meet someone in a similar situation, perhaps in their own home and try to arrange this. This kind of chat can be particularly useful where carers are having difficulties coming to terms with their particular circumstance or face particularly acute problems.

The questions below suggest that you reflect on the way your organisation currently meets the emotional needs of carers.

REVIEWING CURRENT PROVISION

- What assumptions are made in your organisation about the emotional needs of carers? For example:
  - is time allocated for staff to deal with carers' emotional needs?
  - do staff discuss this issue?
  - if they do, what kinds of views do they hold on it?
- What recognition does your organisation give to carers' emotional needs in:
  - policy guidelines?
  - the provision of special services?
  - training?
- Think about one or two individual carers known to you, how their emotional needs have been met in the past, and how they are met at the moment.

– what kinds of things do they want to talk about? (For instance, becoming a carer, feelings about caring, the condition of the person cared for, marital problems, financial worries.)

– who do they prefer to talk to? (For instance, a friend, a family member, a professional worker, another carer.)

– what settings do they prefer to talk in? (For instance, at home, outside the home, in a group, individually.)

– what difficulties do they have in getting these kinds of needs met?

– what training or instructions would help workers meet these needs?

You may find it helpful to discuss these questions with a colleague and to seek the views of carers.

SUGGESTIONS FOR ACTION Listed below are fourteen suggestions for action. Some require a change in individual attitude and practice. Some require the development of greater sensitivity. Some need management or policy decisions about the allocation of time or resources.

- Identify those already in practice in your organisation or local areas
- Identify any you would like to see implemented
- For any you would like to see implemented, think about
  – how feasible this would be
  – who should be responsible for implementation
  – what you could do to start the process of implementation. Depending on the idea and your position this could mean anything from discussing the issue with colleagues and canvassing support through to formulating a proposal or allocating resources.

■ **Review guidelines for home visits** ensuring they include a reminder to set aside time for talking to the carer.

■ **Arrange periodic health checks** by general practitioners. These provide an important chance to talk, as well as to monitor the health and well-being of the carer. The special health risks entailed in caring need to be taken seriously. A dismissive attitude towards carers' health problems should be avoided, for instance attributing feelings of anxiety and depression to the menopause.

■ **Refer carers to appropriate sources of help,** preferably to a named person within an organisation. However sympathetic most service providers might be, their concern is inevitably divided between the carer and the person needing care. It is difficult for carers to talk to them about negative feelings or about decisions which involve a clear conflict of interest. In some cases, there will be a need for a social worker for the carer. In others, someone in a voluntary organisation may be better able to help.

■ **Review the training** of all those who work closely with carers. This is not simply a matter of reminding people to try to be helpful. They may need help in thinking through the kinds of questions which need to be asked, for instance not simply 'How is your mother?' but 'How are you getting on with her? Was it always a difficult relationship?'

■ **Establish a counselling service for carers.** Because of their professional focus on the problems of coping with illness and disability, community psychiatric nurses and hospital social workers may be in a good position to do this. An open access arrangement would provide the flexibility and quick response that carers need. Referrals should also be made by other professionals. Hospital staff, for example, might refer carers of discharged patients, enabling them to discuss the implications of caring early on.

■ **Keep yourself informed** about the national and local voluntary organisations concerned with specific conditions that offer counselling and advice to sufferers and their families. Relate (formerly the Marriage Guidance Council) and the Samaritans are particularly well-known here, providing expert counselling through carefully trained volunteers. CancerLink offers someone to talk to about coping with cancer. Some organisations provide counselling via the telephone (see below).

■ **Establish a carers' directory** for use by carers and professionals, listing all organisations and the type of help and support they can provide.

■ **Set up a carers' centre.** Carers' centres which provide information should also be responsive to those who just want to talk. Providing friendly contact and support for lonely carers is an important part of their function. The Wallasey Carers Centre incorporates a comfortably furnished lounge where carers can drop in for a cup of tea and a chat. Some carers who already know each other use the lounge as a meeting point. Others who come in for information also want someone to talk to. The staff make sure that someone is on hand to sit down and take time to talk.

■ **Establish a telephone link.** This can be important for carers who are unable to get out. Although many of the calls may be for practical help or information, a query often provides a peg on which to hang a discussion of more personal problems. The Signpost project in Stockport offers a confidential helpline for carers, staffed mainly by volunteers, about half of whom are ex-carers. The development of listening skills is an important aspect of volunteers' training. Oldham Health Authority has set up a Carers' Linkline. Most of the volunteers are carers or ex-carers and there is also a youth line for young carers. Many voluntary organisations focussed on specific health problems provide some telephone advice. The British Association for Cancer United Patients (BACUP) provides an information and advice line staffed by trained cancer nurses. Action for Research into Multiple Sclerosis (ARMS) has a telephone counselling link.

■ **Support carers' groups by offering resources** such as the use of a room in the social services department, or help in finding premises. Groups may also need some financial support, such as small grants to run a newsletter or to help members get to meetings.

■ **Provide information to carers** about carers' groups and how to contact them.

■ **Facilitate membership of carers' groups** by helping to solve transport or sitting difficulties. Links with an existing sitting service might be useful here. A sitting scheme run by Bradford Social Services Department, for instance, offers extra sitting hours, over and above the normal weekly allocation, to carers who wish to attend a carers' group.

■ **Help carers to make contact with each other** individually. Local contacts are best. One person in the next street may prove more valuable than a list of ten carers scattered over a wide area.

DEVELOPING POLICY

It may be helpful to draw together some principles for policy making in this area. Listed below are some suggestions which could be added to and amended to fit local circumstances – you may find it helpful to discuss these ideas with colleagues.

Policy statements

Policies should recognise carers' need for opportunities to clarify and express their feelings and to share the emotional burdens of caring, including grief over the possible decline and loss of the person cared for. Carers also need time to explore their expectations of themselves and what they can reasonably expect from others.

- Policies should ensure that carers are given opportunities to talk about their needs with staff in an atmosphere of safety and trust.
- Specialist counselling should be available, and adequately funded, to help with particular crises and problems.

- There should be a policy commitment to support both carers' centres and carers' goups. Carers' centres offer information, a friendly welcome and contact with other carers. Carers' groups offer a unique source of support and friendship.

Organisation

- Talking with carers should not be the exclusive province of one profession or group. All those who give services should be approachable and supportive. Carers should be able to choose who to confide in.
- Clear plans should be made about how carers will be supported and time set aside for talking with them.
- Guidelines for staff in contact with carers should ensure that they think about carers' needs as well as those of the people needing care.
- Carers should be informed about all ways of gaining emotional support.
- Statutory authorities should give financial help and other support to carers' groups. They should also help carers to attend, for instance, through help with transport and sitting.

Training

- All workers in regular contact with carers should be helped to understand the nature and strains of the caring relationship. They should be given training in how to listen to carers, and how to cope with discussions of feelings.
- Professionals who set up or work with carers' groups should be given training in groupwork skills.

Setting up a carers' group

Anyone organising a carers' group should ensure that it is provided in a comforting and welcoming atmosphere. Basic requirements are a warm, private room with comfortable chairs, including high-backed chairs for people with back problems. Food and drink help people to feel welcome and relaxed. Volunteers may be useful, for instance to provide hot meals at meetings.

It is important to ensure that the group provides what carers want. Some may seek only tea and a chat. Others may prefer a more structured programme. A specific topic provides a focus for a meeting and a starting point from which carers can open out. Explicit assurances of confidentiality are important. People must be able to express themselves freely, for instance about violent feelings, without fear of retribution. This should be discussed with any professionals involved in a group, working out strategies to ensure support is offered to vulnerable carers without compromising their trust and sense of privacy.

The Barnet Voluntary Service Council set up a number of groups in different areas of the authority, including in clinics and day centres. In Northwood, a night sister at the Northwood and Pinner Cottage Hospital set up a support group for the carers of new referrals for respite care. Its members have become friends and now help each other informally.

In Bristol, a patient participation group attached to a local general practice set up a carers' group in a health centre, with the doctors' backing. It is led by the chairperson of the association, who is a social worker at another health centre.

Of course, many groups are set up either wholly independently or with the help of one of the national carers' organisations (see Useful Organisations).

The Self Help and Carers Support Unit, Hull

The Hull Council for Voluntary Service employs a carers' support worker to develop carers' groups throughout the city. These are open to all carers, but in practice, the majority of carers in the group will be caring for middle aged or elderly people, perhaps because other carers have alternative sources of support. The groups are organised around a twelve-week structured course, involving talks by professionals on topics chosen by carers themselves in the course of discussion with the support worker in preliminary home visits. Liaison with local social services teams is instigated at the planning stage, promoting referrals of carers and arranging access to meeting rooms and facilities for alternative care of the dependent person. Links with day centres and luncheon clubs have also been developed, providing a further source of 'sitting' while carers attend a group.

Groups are run by three workers, each with a clear role. One concentrates on providing comfort and reassurance, another acts to stimulate discussion, and the third feeds back information and creates opportunities for people to participate. This level of professional input seems necessary, because many carers have low morale and confidence. Three of the four groups launched to date have continued to meet on a self-help basis, beyond the initial 12-week course, with a lower level of involvement from the support worker.

The project has given priority to areas where there are high concentrations of elderly people but poor community facilities and limited transport. For many carers, the groups provide their only opportunity for social contact and a break. It is felt that they have gained improved confidence and self esteem, as well as more realistic expectations of themselves.

PROVIDING INFORMATION

*'It's not just that I don't know what's available,
but I don't even know what questions to ask.'*

**Information about available benefits and services as well as
how to cope with the particular condition of the person
cared for.**

Carers need information about all the services that might help them, about the condition of the person they care for and about the task of caring and the skills associated with it.

Many carers do not know what questions to ask. Some carers manage to find out what they need to know and sometimes become more knowledgeable than the professionals who are their first port of call, but most find it very difficult. Because carers are often isolated, or simply very wrapped up in day-to-day processes of caring, particular efforts are needed to get information to them. Those working with carers need to be one step ahead about possible information needs. They should not assume that because a carer appears competent, he or she will automatically get what is needed.

A service which met carers' needs for information adequately would include a greater understanding by all workers of the kind of information needed. Special publicity and information services would be developed and all workers would take greater responsibility for providing information.

**DEVELOPING A BETTER
SERVICE**

What information is needed?

Carers need information about the condition of the person cared for. Many carers get little such information. Medical professionals often make a judgement – as well as how to get these. They may need to know how to contact their local welfare rights officer, a bereavement counsellor or the local continence adviser. Some may need legal advice. They may also want information about local self-help groups, relevant voluntary organisations or even sources of leisure well outside the world of caring.

Carers need information about the condition of the person cared for. Many carers get little such information. Medical professionals often make a judgement that families do not really want to know. This may come from concern to protect the family from pain or from reluctance to be the bearer of bad news. But carers themselves say they do want to know. In the absence of information, there is a tendency to imagine the worst. They also feel they cannot provide the best care, nor plan ahead for their own lives, when they do not know what to expect.

Individual professionals, particularly doctors, should think about carers' needs as well as those of the person needing care. Both should be given as much information as possible. Where the diagnosis or prognosis is uncertain, the carer should be told. In some families, there may be concern over confidentiality. The person cared for may not want the condition discussed with anyone else and this must be respected. This problem can largely be avoided by giving information in very general terms, explaining the normal prognosis of a person with the condition.

Professionals need to remember that they should provide information about the condition on more than one occasion. Probably the worst time is at the point of diagnosis. The carer is likely to be in too great a state of shock to absorb much information. Written information, which can be taken home and read in a moment of quiet, can play a key role here.

Carers need information about specific skills they need for caring. Some skills are needed to protect themselves, such as how to lift someone without causing damage to their own back. Others are more important to the person who needs care, for instance, some speech therapy, so that progress gained throughout the year is not lost over a holiday. Some simple skills can be explained by the professionals with whom carers come into contact, but others may be too difficult to learn quickly. It is important to refer carers to other sources of help in this case. Health visitors can offer clinic sessions to carers of older people, as well as of children, to learn skills.

A job for everyone

Providing information should not be seen as the responsibility of only one organisation or person. It should be something that everyone remembers to do. A GP, for example, after completing an examination of a man following a stroke, should turn to his wife and ask if she has looked into entitlement to benefit. Home helps should ask if carers have seen a catalogue of nursing aids. This means thinking about what carers might want to know, and knowing either the answer or how to find out. Giving information is not something which is done just once. It involves checking and rechecking, as people's needs change.

Those who provide formal services to people with disabilities should think actively about the information needs of their carers. Day centres for elderly people or people with learning difficulties, for instance, should have someone who serves as an information officer. So, too, should hostels and homes providing short-term residential care. Special schools should be aware of parents' needs and offer information about benefits and local services. This should be done on a regular basis, as part of a normal routine. People who can serve as interpreters should be available to help carers who speak little English (see Chapter 3).

Setting up special information services can be very helpful. (See suggestions below.) All such services need to be well publicised. They should be well known to all people coming into contact with carers – GPs and social workers, staff at day centres and those providing residential care. The local post office could play a key role here, as so many people, particularly pensioners, tend to call in there. For black and ethnic minority carers, it is important to get information out to the places where they congregate. Places of worship may be useful here, including mosques, churches and temples.

All information should be produced in simple language, without jargon. Photographs and illustrations should show people from black and ethnic minorities as well as white people. Translations should be provided.

REVIEWING INFORMATION SERVICES

The questions below suggest that you reflect on the current provision of information to carers in your area.

- How do different organisations and establishments approach the question of information for carers? What priority is given to providing information? How effective are they in providing information?
- What special information and publicity services exist for carers in your area? How up to date and relevant is the information they provide?
- How is information organised in your establishment or organisation? Who has

access to it? How easy is it to get access? How is it disseminated and who by? How often is it up-dated?

- Think about one or two individual carers known to you.
  - what kind of information have they needed and when?
  - how have their information needs been established and then met?
  - how reliable and helpful have they found the information they have received?

You may find it helpful to discuss these questions with a colleague and to seek the views of carers.

SUGGESTIONS FOR ACTION Listed below are fifteen suggestions that could help to develop a better information service for carers. Some are a question of a change of attitude or practice. Many can be carried out with minimal resources. Some require a change of policy and a few need substantial resources.

- Identify those already in practice in your organisation or local area.
- Identify any you would like to see implemented
- For any you would like to see implemented think about:
  - how feasible this would be
  - who should be responsible for implementation
  - what you could do to start the process of implementation. Depending on the idea and your position this could mean anything from discussing the issue with colleagues and canvassing support to formulating a proposal or allocating resources.

■ **Set up a Carers' Centre.** This can bring together disparate strands of information under one roof and at the end of a telephone. It may also encourage local carers' groups to come together to discuss issues of common concern. Ideally, a carers' centre should involve at least one full-time worker, with possible additional part-time help. In some areas, a commitment to work with black and ethnic minority carers is essential. A carers' centre should have a central base, easily accessible to anyone going to the high street shops. This would also enable it to function as a drop-in centre, where carers could share their problems and have a chat. It could be housed in the premises of an established organisation, like a council for voluntary service or in a side room of a day centre or within a hospital. Finance should be sought on a permanent basis. The Carers' Centre in Wallasey (see box) is probably the best known, but there are others, such as that set up in Hove, East Sussex, which includes a drop-in facility.

■ **Create a post for a carers' worker.** This person can play a key role in publicising carers' issues throughout an area. He or she might produce a newsletter (see below), and write articles for the local newspapers, helping to keep carers on the public agenda. The most well-known carers' worker is in Sutton. In the London Borough of Camden, one social worker spends one day a week in this role.

■ **Set up carers' information displays.** These can be run for a day or a week. The Community Care Special Action Project in Birmingham intend to run a series of carers' weeks in different areas of the authority, with displays publicising local service and voluntary organisations. They will include particular attention to the needs and concerns of black and ethnic minority carers.

■ **Set up a mobile information unit** with some of the information which would exist in a carers' centre. This has the advantage of getting out to where carers are. It could be set up for a half day or more in health centres, day centres or even shopping centres. A fixed timetable might be set for visits, so that carers would know when the unit would be visiting their area. It could also be taken to the meetings of carers' groups. The Caring Together project in Stockport organised a mobile exhibition about aids and other support services. This was found to be especially successful in large shops. The Signpost project in Stockport has a bus which serves as a mobile information unit. It spends several months in an area, providing information and helping to develop self-help and other community initiatives. The presence of the bus, combined with good advance publicity, helps to raise awareness of carers' issues.

■ **Set up a telephone helpline.** This is particularly vital for carers who cannot get out of the house. A helpline can be assisted by an outreach worker who visits carers in their homes. Volunteers might be able to help here. The C.A.R.E.S. scheme (Carers Advice and Resource Establishment in Sandwell) has recently set up a telephone advice and information service, housed in a church.

■ **Write a carers' handbook** providing information on all sources of help to carers in an area. It should also give some general information, such as where to complain about services. The problem with handbooks is that they are costly to produce and may quickly become out of date. 'Caring at Home', a handbook produced by the King's Fund Informal Caring Programme can be customised by local agencies to provide information relevant to their own area. This may be cheaper than developing a local handbook from scratch. Both North Yorkshire and the London Borough of Lewisham have prepared good handbooks, with a great deal of information for carers. In Stockport, the Council for Voluntary Service and Caring Together project produced a small handbook which will be regularly updated.

■ **Produce a newsletter.** This may prove particularly cost effective. A newsletter can provide information to carers in a chatty and useful way. There are many good examples. The newsletter prepared by the Sutton branch of the Carers National Association deserves a particular mention; it is published monthly and circulated widely to carers and professionals. It includes a report on meetings, information on local services and changes in what is available.

■ **Produce simple fact sheets** covering specific problems in caring. These can set out detailed instructions for dealing with a particular condition, and be made available to carers as required. The Neighbourhood Care Project in Swindon produced some useful sheets of this kind. It is important however that fact sheets are not substituted for regular chats. Professionals should remember to discuss the situation with carers on a regular basis.

■ **Produce a carers' pack,** incorporating a number of such sheets (in languages other than English where appropriate). This should not be so large that it seems daunting. Leicester Rights Centre developed a useful carers' pack.

■ **Use local newspapers and radio** to get information to carers' homes. These can inform carers about help available in the area, including meetings of individual carers' groups, and can be particularly useful for getting information to ethnic minority carers. The media have been well used by the Care for the Carers Project in East Sussex.

■ **Help voluntary organisations** which focus on particular health problems or disabilities to provide detailed information to carers. For example, the newsletter of Contact a Family (support groups for families whose children have special needs) is called 'Share an Idea'. Citizens Advice Bureaux are also in a good position to provide such information. An information, advice and advocacy project for carers, including outreach work, has recently been set up within the CAB service of the London Borough of Sutton, including outreach work. The Hazel Grove CAB in Stockport has a carers' home visitor.

■ **Support carers' groups in giving information.** This can be done partly through members, who are often very familiar with local services and know who to contact, for what kinds of help. They may also have a wealth of tips on how to cope with a particular problem. Many also provide talks about local services or the benefit system. Local professionals should offer their services to groups as a speaker. This gives information and allows you to become a known person with a familiar face, who can help groups follow up information needs at a later date.

■ **Keep up to date with information produced by national organisations.** Some, such as the MS Society, include pages for carers in their newsletter. Translations should be available. Carers can be encouraged to write for such information. Professionals in regular contact with carers should keep samples to show people who inquire and up-to-date names and addresses, ideally of a local contact and the headquarters office.

■ **Find out about local resource centres.** Some organisations for people with disabilities run local resource centres, which have detailed information about their specific condition and how to care for people with it. The Care and Resource Centre run by the Birmingham Branch of the Alzheimers Disease Society, for instance, provides information to professionals and carers. Some organisations, like the British Red Cross, run courses and training on such matters as lifting and bathing.

■ **Encourage carers to use telephone health information services.** These provide tape recorded messages on specific health problems, from life-threatening problems like AIDS and cancer to chronic annoyances like skin problems and sleeplessness. One set up by the College of Health is called 'Healthline' and costs only the charge of a local telephone call. Other commercial lines have also been developed. They are readily accessible from a carer's own home and have the advantage of being cheap and confidential. Information ranges from a carer's own needs to ways of coping with a particular condition.

DEVELOPING POLICY

It may be helpful to draw together some principles for policy making in this area. Listed below are some suggestions which could be added to and amended to fit local circumstances. You may find it useful to discuss this list with colleagues.

Policy statements

- Policy makers should recognise that carers are often unaware of the benefits and services open to them. Policies should aim to increase the information available through a variety of means.
- Policy makers should draw up guidelines about the dilemma of giving information to carers about the condition of the person needing care and the prognosis. Carers need full information, but this may conflict with confidentiality for the person cared for. These guidelines should be made known to staff.

Organisation

- The effective dissemination of information to carers requires a number of different strategies. All staff who come into contact with carers should see it as their brief to inform carers about local services and benefits. They should inform themselves about what is available, including help from voluntary organisations.
- Carers' centres, telephone helplines or mobile units should be set up, providing a focal point for information to carers.
- Statutory authorities should help voluntary organisations who want to establish such centres, with finance and support.
- There should be someone available to serve as an advocate for carers who need one.
- Written information should be provided to carers through newsletters, handbooks and other means with translations provided where necessary.
- Carers should be included in case conferences and meetings wherever possible.
- All facilities for treating people cared for should be accessible to carers.
- Wherever possible carers should be given information on the nature of the condition and the prognosis. This includes information on how to manage the care, regularly reviewed and updated.
- Carers should have access to specialists.

Training

- All those who work with carers should be trained to understand carers' information needs and how to meet them.
- Professionals should be trained in how to listen to and communicate with carers, treating them as partners and equals, often with great expertise in their own right.
- Those with specialist skills should be trained to share these skills with carers, as well as to teach them general skills such as lifting.
- Carers should be offered training in practical and nursing skills, as well as advice on how to manage demanding or confused behaviour.

The Wallasey Carers Care Centre, Council for Voluntary Service

The Carers Care Centre, run by the Wallasey Council for Voluntary Service, provides a place where carers can go for information and support, as well as practical help. Set up in 1986, it is open every day of the week: 9.30am to 9.30pm on weekdays, but shorter hours at weekends. There are two full-time staff, plus 12 ancillary workers employed on a shift basis. It has a welcoming environment with comfortable armchairs so that carers can drop in for a chat. Staff are available to discuss problems and will refer carers to appropriate agencies for help, such as the local Citizens Advice Bureau. Access to many local professionals and back-up support from the CVS is essential to the success of the Centre. There is a strong emphasis on confidentiality. Staff provide not only a listening ear with regard to carers' problems but also advice about how to approach local service providers. A permanent exhibition of aids is displayed in its window.

The Centre serves as more than just an information centre. It also runs an incontinence laundry service, offering collection and delivery. Some carers also use the centre as a convenient and comfortable place to meet other carers. The Centre is owned by the local Council for Voluntary Service, but staff are employed through the MSC Community Programme.

INCOME AND EMPLOYMENT

'I never thought it would come to this. I feel like a pauper.'

An income which covers the costs of caring and does not preclude carers taking employment or sharing care with other people.

UNDERSTANDING THE ISSUES

Caring costs. In addition to its physical and emotional strains caring can impose great financial burdens. For some people this is temporary, but for others caring can mean permanent poverty. This chapter outlines some of the financial implications of caring. It describes some of the costs that may be incurred. It explores some of the assumptions about family roles and responsibilities that may influence individual decisions and the decisions of policy makers. It discusses problems in the benefits systems and service provision and the difficulties some families may face in claiming benefits and requesting services.

The costs of caring

Disability and illness often bring additional costs which can be substantial. For example, extra heating and washing, necessary for a doubly incontinent elderly person, produce enormous energy bills. Household budgets may have to stretch to extra bedding and clothing, special furniture, continence equipment and aids or adaptations to the home. A telephone may need to be installed. The car may need to be adapted. Taxi fares may have to be found if public transport cannot be used. Jobs such as childcare and DIY that the carer used to do may now have to be paid for. Money for respite care may have to be found. The new community charge will also weigh heavily on households with a carer.

The effect on employment

Caring also creates or compounds disadvantages in employment. Carers who remain in work often change their job in order to fit in with the needs of the person they care for. This may mean taking a job with lower pay or fewer prospects or opting for part-time, temporary or casual work. Carers are also at a disadvantage if they have to take unpaid leave or are unable to do overtime because of the situation at home. Sometimes pension entitlement and promotion prospects are affected.

People who are unemployed, in low-paid or part-time work are often seen, or see themselves, as the obvious choice when a carer is needed in the family. Women are particularly likely to give up work and career prospects in order to care.

Assumptions

Many common assumptions about caring and family relationships work to the financial disadvantage of carers. These assumptions can be found in government policy, in the attitudes of professional workers and in the feelings and beliefs of carers and their families. For example:

- Caring is usually seen as a matter for individual families to deal with. It is only partially seen as a collective responsibility that society should make some provision for. The assumption is that the family will find someone to care, regardless of the financial or personal cost.
- The work of caring is not highly valued. It is assumed that because carers want to care they do not need payment for what they do or compensation for what they lose.
- Caring is often seen as a natural part of women's role and it is assumed that they do not need help. Several studies have found that in comparable situations local authorities allocate more home helps to people being cared for by men than by women.

Obstacles to claiming benefits

Difficulties also exist within families that can increase financial problems. Many carers share the common assumption that caring is their responsibility and may feel reluctant to claim the benefits and services that are available. Some see claiming as charity. Some are put off by the complexity and unpleasantness of claiming. In some situations there is in-built conflict between carers and those they care for. The Severe Disability Premium cannot be paid to anyone living with a fit carer or to anyone who is getting Invalid Care Allowance on the basis of caring for them. If one gets ICA the other cannot get SDP and vice versa.

These difficulties require sensitive help if families are to overcome reluctance to claim and find a solution that helps everyone.

Problems with the benefits system

At present, there is patchy and inadequate social security provision for people with disabilities and their carers. Most of the available benefits are restricted in one way or another so that they apply only to some groups of carers, do not help many of the poorest and force others to choose between work and caring. The main benefits which are directly associated with disability and which carers need to know about are Attendance Allowance, Invalid Care Allowance, Mobility Allowance and Community Care Grants.

Because it is not the recognised responsibility of any person or profession to give carers information about the benefits system, many carers are unaware that they may be eligible. Though benefit levels are decided at national level, local workers can help carers greatly by passing on information, giving them the appropriate forms and encouraging them to understand that they have rights to these allowances.

Some people may also be interested in the work of the 'Caring Costs' coalition. This is a group who are working on proposals for a new system of benefits for all carers. They propose that there should be a carers' benefit to replace the earnings of carers of working age and a carers allowance paid to all carers towards the extra cost of caring. A partial carers' benefit would be paid to carers in part-time work and other measures taken to help carers who wish to combine caring with employment, for example, a much higher earnings disregard.

Problems in service provision

In the current climate there is increased pressure on local authorities and voluntary agencies to charge for community services that used to be provided free. Charges for services such as home helps, meals on wheels, short term care in residential establishments and laundry services put additional pressure on hard-pressed family incomes and may restrict the take up of much needed services. Charging for relief care can prevent carers from taking a much needed break.

There are also many anomalies in the charges for similar services levied by different agencies. For example, respite care provided in a hospital is free, but a short stay in a residential home has to be paid for. This incentive to use health services is inconsistent with a policy of providing care in homely surroundings and is likely to affect take up of community services that are charged for.

Local authorities should review their policies on charging, eliminating any charges that do not cover the costs of collection and introducing a sliding scale related to income where charging is unavoidable.

The questions below suggest that you reflect on what you and your agency can do to help carers obtain an adequate income.

REVIEWING YOUR ROLE

- How familiar are you with the welfare benefits system? Are you able to help carers claim what they are entitled to?
- What are your agency's policies on charging for services? If charges are made, how are these set? What is the effect of charging on take up of services?
- How helpful is your agency in helping carers maintain their income – for instance by providing cover that allows them to work?
- Think about one or two individual carers known to you
  – has becoming a carer affected their income?
  – what effect does caring have on their ability to work and their career prospects?
  – what extra costs has caring brought for them?
  – how easy do they find it to pay for services they need?
  – do they need information about welfare benefits and help in claiming them?

You may find it helpful to discuss these questions with a colleague and to seek the views of carers.

Local agencies cannot change social security policy as this is determined at central level but they can review their own policies to ensure that carers obtain the full range of benefits to which they are entitled. They can also consider the impact charges for local services will have on carers' incomes. As employers, they can recognise carers in their workforce and implement policies which enable carers of working age to keep their jobs or return to work if they wish to.

SUGGESTIONS FOR ACTION

Listed below are six suggestions for action that may improve carers' financial situation.

- Identify those already in practice in your organisation or local area
- Identify any you would like to see implemented

- For any you would like to see implemented, think about:
  - how feasible this would be
  - what you could do to start the process of implementation. Depending on the idea and your position this could mean anything from discussing the issue with colleagues and canvassing support through to formulating a proposal or allocating resources.

■ **Reappraise assumptions about costs** of caring and who should bear them by:
- reading the literature on the subject
- consulting carers' organisations and groups
- raising the issue in staff meetings or training exercises

■ **Support campaigns** to improve benefits for carers by:
- endorsing representations to government
- offering assistance in kind or cash to voluntary organisations who wish to increase awareness of carers' financial difficulties

■ **Increase benefits take-up** by:
- producing and distributing information (leaflets, information days, face to face advice from front line professionals)
- mounting special take up campaigns
- providing training for staff about the benefits system
- encouraging staff to act as mediators or advocates on carers' behalf with local social security offices
- assisting carers and their relatives to buy in services using all the available benefits for which they are eligible. Special attention should be given to Community Care Grants in Social Fund – a new element of Income Support replacing Supplementary Benefit

■ **Review and modify charges for services** by:
- examining charging anomalies (compare charges for similar services levied by the health service, local authority and other agencies)
- where discretion in the level of charging is allowed, consulting consumer groups about what they regard as fair and reasonable
- where charges are made, creating bands of charges consistent with income levels, ensuring that no charge is made where people are dependent on social security or
- levying low flat-rates to all

■ **Enable carers to keep their jobs by providing:**
- night cover
- early morning help in the home

- meals service
- day care for disabled relatives (see Chapter 4)
- ■ **Act as a good employer** by
- ensuring that welfare and personnel officers are aware of carers' needs
- making agreements on family and compassionate leave (a set number of days per year)
- setting up workplace support groups
- helping carers in the workforce secure assistance in the local community

---

DEVELOPING POLICY

It may be helpful to draw together some principles for policy making in this area. Listed below are some suggestions which could be added to and amended to fit local circumstances. You may find it helpful to discuss these ideas with colleagues.

Policy statements

The major responsibility for income maintenance rests with the DHSS who provide benefits to people who need care and, to a lesser extent, their carers. There is a need to review the benefit system with respect to carers, to explore a carers' benefit and other welfare payments that would cover the costs of care. The conditions surrounding benefits for carers should not preclude them from taking employment or from sharing care with other people.

- It should be the explicit aim of local policy to help carers get the full range of benefits to which they (and the people they care for) are entitled. They should also minimise charges for respite services and other local help. Efforts should be made to increase carers' opportunities to gain or maintain employment.
- Recent changes in the social security system raise important issues for carers and the people they care for. Policy-makers should familiarise themselves with these changes and consult carers about the implications for local services.

Organisation

Local campaigns should be launched to ensure that carers and the people they care for get the benefits to which they are entitled. They should include information, and help in making claims, and dealing with assessments or appeals. Welfare rights officers should be available to carers.

- Local service providers should earmark funds that can be used for carers by middle management and front line workers.
- Day care services should be sufficiently flexible in their hours to help working

carers. Care attendant schemes should also provide cover over sufficient hours to enable carers to work.

- Employers should encourage carers to take jobs or remain in employment where they wish. This means providing flexibility in working hours and working conditions.

Training

- All people who come into contact with carers should be trained to have some familiarity with the benefit system, to know what benefits are available and how to claim them.

Helping carers to claim benefits: the Bexley Community Care Scheme

The Bexley Community Care Scheme was started in 1984 by the Social Services Department to develop alternatives to residential care for frail old people.

The scheme is based on a combination of case management, expert professional help and DHSS benefits. It is founded on the belief that carers should have maximum control over their own situation and that this is best acquired through knowledge and money. It has therefore given high priority to securing all benefits to which the people they care for are entitled. The Scheme applies for benefits on carers'

behalf: bridging loans are offered to pay for immediate help. Carers are seen as the best judge of their own needs and can buy in help as they wish. This may be from paid neighbours, care attendants and others found through word of mouth, leafletting or advertisements in local shops.

The Community Care Scheme, in collaboration with local voluntary agencies and the DHSS, also set up a working party on benefits to simplify the claiming of benefits. It has worked particularly closely with one self-help group in the area, known as ACE (Association of Carers for the Elderly).

Carers and work: a charter by voluntary organisations

This charter was drawn up by voluntary organisations in conjunction with carers.

Voluntary organisations work closely with carers. We have direct experience of their needs. We know the pressures they have to cope with every day. We know the guilt they often feel, either about letting down their dependant or letting down their employer because of an unforeseen crisis at home.

This is why we have joined together with carers who work to draw up this five-point charter. We believe that good employers and unions should all be able to implement this plan in full, as part of positive policies for carers in the workplace. It should provide a basis for action and agreement by employers, unions and voluntary groups:

- *action for carers to help them cope with their caring responsibilities and give of their best at work as committed employees;*
- *agreement on how best to provide for a growing proportion of workers with responsibilities for caring for dependants in the home*
- **Workplace Support Groups**
  In every workplace those with caring responsibilities should be invited to set up a support group with the involvement of trade unions. As a first step, a letter might be sent to all staff, inviting those who are carers to attend an informal meeting.

  It is usually best if an employee is given specific responsibility for servicing the group — arranging for outside speakers and ensuring good liaison and help from the local Social Services Department, the local carers' organisations, the Crossroads Care Attendant Scheme, and so on. Employers often find that the Personnel or Welfare Officer, or an Occupational Nurse, is the best person to take on these responsibilities.

- **Flexible Working Hours**
  No amount of good planning can prevent difficulties and crises from cropping up unforeseen. That is why flexibility is the hallmark of an effective policy for carers. It also benefits employers if carers can make up for lost time later, when they can perform better than they do under stress. In many workplaces there are now flexible arrangements for childcare. Now is the time to extend this flexibility to all carers in employment.
- **Family and Compassionate Leave**
  Flexible hours make it a lot easier for carers to cope with a short crisis. For more serious crises they should be entitled to unpaid or even paid leave.

  In every workplace and establishment, a specific agreement should cover the needs of carers for family or compassionate leave. Some employers have already made agreements for up to 5 or 10 days leave each year to be granted on compassionate grounds to those with caring responsibilities.

- **Links with the Local Community**
  Workplace support groups should make sure they have good links with local voluntary and community organisations. They can do a lot to help, for example by providing transport to visit dependants in hospital, or advising on how best to approach statutory services for help.
- **Assistance to the Local Community**
  In some areas, voluntary groups provide a range of services for carers, such as home care schemes, day centres and sitting services.

  Employers can do much to assist voluntary organisations with these schemes either through direct financial assistance or technical support. This, in turn, should help voluntary groups to extend the services they can make available at the workplace.

ALTERNATIVES TO FAMILY CARE

'I don't want them to think that I am pushing my child on.
I want them to come forward and say
'we would like to have her'. Then I should be happy.'

Opportunities to explore alternatives to family care, both for the immediate and the long term future.

DILEMMAS OF ALTERNATIVE CARE

Alternative care is a very sensitive issue. It is a subject on which most carers feel deeply, and in many cases think about often. Yet it is rarely raised directly either by them or others. Carers have widely differing views on this question and many are highly ambivalent. Those who are trying to maintain paid employment and those with limited living space may be particularly anxious to find an alternative arrangement. The subject is complicated by the fact that it is one on which a carer's needs and those of the person cared for may well diverge.

This issue confronts carers when they first find themselves in the caring role and continues throughout the time that they are caring. Many feel that they do not have a choice in whether they become or remain carers. It is what they want and ought to do. Others would prefer another solution, if a suitable arrangement could be found, either from the beginning or from some point when they can no longer cope. Some carers are elderly and know that at some point they will need to find alternative care, for instance for a son with severe learning difficulties. Some become very worn down and unable to carry on. Others do not want to find themselves trapped and consider the only solution an early opting out.

A key question here is what is best for the person needing care. This differs greatly from one family to another. A young person with a physical disability, for example, could live independently and seeking an alternative arrangement will seem a good course. Indeed, it may well be what he or she really wants. In contrast, where the condition of the person needing care is likely to deteriorate, a move is a particularly difficult decision. Furthermore, there are families where it is simply inappropriate, for instance those with a dying spouse. There is also the matter of timing. A move may be sought for the immediate future or only for the longer term, 'after I'm gone'. In either case, a fundamental issue is the extent and quality of alternative care.

Sufficient provision

It is important that there is sufficient provision for carers, and those they care for, to have a choice in taking this decision. Local authorities, health authorities and voluntary organisations need to provide residential care suitable for the full range of people needing care – young and old, those with severe and mild disabilities, those who require nursing and those who do not. Increasingly such care is being moved away from hospitals and hostels to smaller community based alternatives geared to individual needs. Independent living schemes and supported housing arrangements for those able to use them should be expanded and arrangements to provide full-time care within the home should be set up. There is also a need for hospices for people who are terminally ill. Such provision needs to be of good quality, sensitive to the needs of residents and accessible to visits by family and friends. The decision to move there should not have to be seen as the last resort.

The need for information

In order to make a good decision carers and the people they care for need information on what is available both locally and further afield. They need to know not only how many places exist and for what kinds of people but also the details of day-to-day care. Many carers may be reluctant to ask for such information. It should be readily available from local organisations, particularly the social services department, and it may need to be provided in different languages.

Carers also need the opportunity to visit local provision probably more than once and at different times of the day. Meeting staff and other residents may be a help, particularly to get the feel of what it is like to live there. Individual homes need to make themselves as accessible as possible. People should feel welcome to visit, to talk, and to walk around (always intruding as little as possible on existing residents' privacy). Where carers speak little English, someone to accompany them on such visits and offer translation is crucial.

Another kind of information comes from direct experience. One means of helping carers and the people they care for explore alternative arrangements is through short stays in the place to which the person needing care would go. This is often recommended to give carers a break (see Chapter 4), but it is suggested here for a different purpose. A trial separation, provides an opportunity to see what it is like to live separately. It also offers a first hand experience of the place.

Someone to talk to

Many carers also need a chance to explore this issue with someone in a dispassionate but sympathetic way. This may be a social worker, a professional counsellor, a carers' support group or a fellow carer faced with a similar decision. What is important is that it is someone with whom the carer feels comfortable. Seeking alternative care is so ridden with complex feelings of guilt and fear of 'putting him away' that it is a very difficult step to take. Even raising the issue can be hard. Carers are likely to be highly sensitive to any suggestion that they are selfish, or failing in their responsibilities. At worst, they may not raise the subject again for years. In some families, the person who needs care may make the situation more difficult by declaring that 'my daughter promised that she will always look after me'. It is essential to check with the carer that this is indeed the plan.

Carers may need continuing support after the person they care for has left in order to talk through the feelings of loss.

Involving the person needing care

Throughout any discussion of this issue, it is important that the person who needs care is fully involved. It should not be assumed that the carer has the power of disposition over someone else's life. Such discussions will differ, of course, depending on the condition of the person needing care. A person with a physical disability, for instance, will want a full say in where he or she will go. A person who is mentally confused, in contrast, may be less able to make a full contribution. Furthermore, it must not be automatically assumed that the care provided by the carer is the best care possible. There will be circumstances where a move is in the best interests of the person needing care. Such issues cannot be determined from the outside, and the needs of all parties to be involved must be recognised.

The questions below suggest that you reflect on the policies and attitudes within your organisation about alternatives to informal care.

- What provision for long term residential care is made by your organisation or in your local area? How are people selected and admitted? What information is provided to carers and prospective residents?
- Do practice guidelines and training give recognition to carers' needs for information and help in facing dilemmas about accepting alternative care?
- Think about one or two individual carers known to you and the difficulties and decisions they have faced or may face in choosing an alternative to informal care
  - what did they need to know?
  - what did they need to talk about?
  - how was the person needing care involved?
  - how satisfactory was the process both for the carer and the person needing care?

You may find it helpful to discuss these questions with a colleague and to seek the views of carers.

Listed below are eight suggestions for improving the opportunities carers have to explore alternatives to family care. Most rely on changes in attitude and practice by workers who help carers and the people they care for to manage this transition.

- Identify those already in practice in your organisation or local area
- Identify any you would like to see implemented
- For any you would like to see implemented, think about:
  - how feasible this would be
  - who would be responsible for implementation
  - what you could do to start the process of implementation. Depending on the idea and your position this could mean anything from discussing the issue with colleagues and canvassing support through to formulating a proposal or allocating resources.

■ **Raise the issue of alternative provision early and often.** It is not enough to do so once and presume the carer will then find it easy to raise again. Be prepared to explore the financial implications of a move to residential care as well.

■ **Develop your knowledge about provision in your area,** statutory, voluntary and private. This is not just its location, but more detailed information so that you can answer some initial questions. Arrange to visit places and get to know local managers. This will make it much easier to discuss what is available and to have some idea of its suitability for particular families. It will also help you to advise carers on the questions they need to ask when they visit.

■ **Encourage discussion of alternative care** at carers support groups and with members of groups for elderly and disabled people. Because carers are often reluctant to raise the issue, this could serve as a catalyst for them to express their feelings with others, perhaps for the first time. Another carer who had made a successful transition might be invited to discuss the issue, focussing the discussion in a very down-to-earth way. Similarly, workshops for carers might include this as one topic (see box).

■ **Produce a handbook** setting out information on the range of local services and including details of residential care and how to find out more. Wolverhampton Metropolitan District Council have prepared a booklet for parents of children with learning difficulties, describing its residential services in some detail and making suggestions to help families prepare themselves for a move.

■ **Produce leaflets about individual homes.** These do not need to be glossy brochures but should set out simply the answers to some of the more common questions.

■ **Display information** about alternative provision at the carers' centre, if one exists. This information should be seen as central and attention called to its existence.

■ **Arrange visits** to local provision making sure there are opportunities to meet staff and residents and time to talk about the visit afterwards.

■ **Arrange short trial stays** as a first step to a longer term move. Offer opportunities to discuss the experience after it has taken place.

Finally it may be helpful to draw together some principles for policy making in this area. Listed below are some suggestions which could be added to and amended to fit local circumstances. You may find it helpful to discuss the ideas with colleagues.

DEVELOPING POLICY

Policy statements

Policy statements should recognise that care by the family is not always best for the person who needs care or for the carer. Some people needing care have no available carer or would like to live away from home. Some carers are unable or unwilling to provide care on a longer-term basis. These issues may arise when care is first needed or after many years of caring. Policies should recognise that caring takes place within a relationship. It should not be seen as an obligation which falls naturally on one person, but rather as a role that evolves through a network of relationships and which ideally might be shared.

- Policy makers should ensure that there is adequate provision of residential care and independent living alternatives, of suitable quality to provide a real choice for carers and the people they care for.
- Residential treatment facilities (including short-term hospital places) should be available for people with mental illness.
- It should be policy to ensure that carers are fully informed about what is available.

Organisation

- Services should be reviewed and extended to provide a range of alternative care and independent living options for elderly and disabled people. These should be well publicised.
- Those working with carers should actively encourage them and the people they care for to discuss the issue of alternative care and to go to see what is available. This should include discussion of people's values and beliefs about caring, enabling carers' expectations of themselves and other people's expectations of them to be clarified. This is particularly important for black and ethnic minority carers, where inappropriate assumptions are often made about the existence of an extended family.
- People working with carers should not put pressure on them to take on or continue the role of caring.
- Short stays away from home should be encouraged to give experience of separation.

Training

- Those working with carers should be trained:
  - to understand the nature of carers' complex feelings about alternative care and to open up discussions with them
  - to review their assumptions about who should provide care, for instance, about the role of women
  - to mediate between carers and the people they care for in discussing difficult issues like alternatives to family care.

Workshop for parents of deaf-blind and rubella handicapped children

As part of its Annual Weekend Away for parents, Sense — The National Deaf-Blind and Rubella Association — ran a workshop to discuss the question of seeking alternative care and 'letting go'. This was run by the organisation's Parents Liaison Officer. Parents were enabled to explore feelings of loss of identity, or actual loss and even bereavement. They also discussed how a child's slow progress into emotional independence challenges parents at every stage — school, respite care, residential care and the last farewell. The parents were at very different stages of letting go.

This workshop was followed up with an article in the Association's newsletter, Talking Sense. This was presented in the guise of a letter:

'Dear fellow parent ... You are right; when you allow your child to go into a residential setting with the knowledge that it may be for life, it is very like a bereavement. The fact that you have allowed it or have agreed with the decision may make it worse.

....There should be, and I am sure will be, a time of discovery and growth, but you will have to allow yourself time to work through the confusion and grief. Preparing for a break is a slow process and you have had little warning. You were seeking a good placement, not preparing for it ...

....This is not really a loss, nor an abandonment. Your child is becoming a young adult and leaving home to find the meaning of community and independent living....'

The letter explored a parent's possible reactions and provided empathy and support. Members were encouraged to respond to it and discuss what it meant to them. Many found this very helpful.

CONSULTATION

*'If only they would ask us
what we want.'*

10

Services designed through consultation with carers at all levels of policy planning.

The most effective way of ensuring that services are responsive to the needs of carers is to involve them in the process of policy formulation and service planning. The diversity of carers means that a very responsive consultative process is required. Formal participation in planning must be complemented by a variety of measures for informal consultation.

Whenever carers are consulted some basic ground rules need to apply. First, the purpose of the consultation should be made clear. Carers need to know why their views are being sought and how information given will be used. Second, the consultation should be genuine. Carers are busy people and they may need reassurance that the time put into consultation is well spent and has a chance of some impact on planning. Retrospective consultation, to validate decisions already taken, is an inappropriate and dishonest use of their time. Finally, the people involved should be given some feedback on the effect of the information gained on policy.

Formal consultation
Carers should be offered direct participation in service committees and planning groups. The carers involved need to know whether they are expected to serve as a representative of a particular constituency or as an informed lay person with special expertise. If it is the former, there is a need for all sides to have an

ENSURING AN APPROPRIATE SERVICE

understanding of whose interests are represented and the limits on the role.

Selecting the people to take part is not always a simple matter. Using carers' own organisations makes this process easier, but there may be conflicts between organisations and questions about the representativeness of those chosen. However these issues are resolved, it is important that the people selected are carers (or in some cases, former carers) and not just speaking on their behalf.

Carers may need help in order to participate effectively. Planners and other professionals may need to adapt their approach, accepting that committee proceedings may become less streamlined due to the participative process.

Carers may need background information on specific issues, so that they understand the history or implications of issues under discussion. Some ethnic minority carers may need the help of an interpreter during meetings and translations of background material. Long serving committee members need to be aware that a carer is likely to feel at a disadvantage. A formal committee can be a confusing place for lay people. Lacking a clear professional status, carers may feel marginal to the main business and assume the role of client rather than partner.

Informal consultation

Informal consultation refers to ways of seeking carers' views outside the formal committee process. This may take many different forms and may be initiated by service-providers or by carers themselves.

A lot can be done by using existing organisations and running special events (see Suggestions for Action below) but it is also important to get the views of more isolated carers who are not in touch with formal services.

This isolation is particularly acute for carers who have recently arrived in this country and others who experience language and cultural barriers. Means should be sought to enable these carers to make their views known. A carers' worker is in a particularly good position to seek them out for discussion.

The role of the voluntary sector

Encouraging the participation of carers should also be viewed as a challenge for the voluntary sector. Those voluntary organisations which deliver services should reflect the interests of carers in the decisions they take. Local development agencies such as councils for voluntary service, which coordinate voluntary groups' response on issues of common concern and take the lead in liaising with statutory bodies, should also promote carers' interests. Those who represent the voluntary sector on joint consultative committees, urban programme consultative bodies and other structures should be well informed about carers' issues. There is a need for these organisations, like statutory bodies, to take an interest in the differing needs of black and ethnic minority carers.

The questions below suggest that you reflect on the consultation processes used in your local area by your own and by other organisations.

REVIEWING CONSULTATION

- Are carers represented on any formal committees?
- Think back over the past year about any consultation events or processes that involved carers. How useful and effective were they for service providers? How useful and effective for the carers? How could they be improved?
- Think about one or two individual carers known to you and how they could best be consulted.
  - what forms of consultation would suit them?
  - what might they find difficult?
  - what changes in attitude and practice might be required by planners or committees in order to involve them fully?

  You may find it helpful to discuss these questions with a colleague and to seek the views of carers.

Listed below are 12 suggestions for improving consultation with carers. They all require commitment to the idea that carers have a right to be consulted and that is the responsibility of service providers fo facilitate their participation.

SUGGESTIONS FOR ACTION

- Identify those already in practice in your organisation or local area.
- Identify those you would like to see implemented.
- For any you would like to see implemented think about:
  - how feasible this would be
  - who would be responsible for implementation
  - what you could do to start the process of implementation. Depending on the idea and your position this could mean anything from discussing the issue with colleagues and canvassing support to formulating a proposal or allocating resources.

■ **Canvass carers' views in a systematic way.** A good example is provided by the Community Care Special Action Project in Birmingham. This involved several rounds of open meetings throughout the city, carried out at regular intervals. The meetings were made as accessible as possible through careful choice of location, help with transport and sitting, and the provision of interpreters for ethnic minority carers. Follow-up interviews were carried out with a sample of participants. The information gained was carefully monitored. Suggestions made by carers were referred to the relevant council department or health authority for action. A similar exercise was carried out by the Stockport Caring Together project and found to be very worthwhile.

■ **Hold special consultative events.** These can prove effective in impressing the concerns of carers on professionals and elected members. They also help carers gain confidence and a sense of solidarity. In Berkshire, for instance, a county-wide meeting was organised by a joint social services and voluntary sector steering group. This gave carers the chance to talk with each other and with a few invited professionals. A carers' charter, setting out proposals for improving local services was subsequently endorsed by the social services committee. This can be an especially useful means of consulting ethnic minority carers. The London Borough of Brent held a day conference for ethnic minority carers.

■ **Hold a carers' information day.** This can inform carers about benefits and services and enable professionals to learn at first hand about the problems carers face. The impact of these occasions can be quite powerful. For senior managers, it may be the first time that they come into direct contact with carers.

■ **Approach carers' groups** for a discussion about local services. Someone responsible for policy should attend, respond to issues and take notes. Both general carers' groups (open to all carers) and groups geared to the needs of one particular set of carers (carers of people with Alzheimers Disease, for instance) should be included. Efforts should be made to include groups of black and ethnic minority carers in such consultations. An annual meeting might be arranged with the Director of Social Services. In North Yorkshire, a conference for carers was one of the events which led to the publication by the social services department of a handbook for carers.

■ **Establish a permanent carers' forum.** These provide regular meetings of carers with service staff, such as social workers. The Leicester Carers' Forum, set up to advise on a national voluntary sector initiative, has continued to meet on a regular basis, drawing together members of carers' groups throughout the city as well as some carers with no previous group involvement. There is also regular liaison with senior management within the social services department. Local forums of this kind can also be the basis for carers to get access to more formal consultation procedures, for example by briefing voluntary sector representatives on joint consultative committees and joint planning teams. Carers' forums need to be adequately resourced and serviced. This is an appropriate task for local development agencies, such as councils of voluntary service, which have experience in supporting special interest groups.

■ **Organise surveys.** These can identify numbers of carers and their circumstances and they can enable service providers to assess services and identify other resources that are needed. A household survey (1 in 5) carried out by Tameside Metropolitan District to discover the size and needs of the carer population, was followed up with in-depth interviews with a sample of carers, including a number of Asian carers. Many valued the opportunity to chat informally, often for the first time, about their situation. A survey exercise on this scale is clearly expensive and time-consuming and will not be thought feasible in every area. More limited surveys of specific groups or neighbourhoods can be a useful mechanism for consultation. Surveys of users of particular services, for instance respite care or care assistants, can be a good means of getting information on their value to consumers. Students could be used here. The North West Schizophrenia Fellowship used an MSc student to research the needs of carers of mentally ill people in the Stockport area.

■ **Offer carers direct participation** in service committees and planning groups, such as joint consultative groups or planning groups for elderly people and people with learning difficulties. To give two examples, parents are well represented on the local Planning Teams for people with learning difficulties in the Exeter District Health Authority and two carers sit on the Joint Care Planning Team in Rochdale (see box).

■ **Provide assistance** to carers so they can participate fully in committees. This would be an appropriate job for a carers' worker. It could also be done by an informed advocate. Some areas now have joint planning coordinators for the voluntary sector (for instance, Manchester, Avon, Leicestershire) whose job it is to brief and support voluntary sector members of formal committees. In other areas, someone in the council for voluntary service (CVS) or community health council (CHC) takes an active interest.

■ **Offer carers some training in committee work.** They will need to know the functions of the body on which they serve and how it relates to other planning and policy-making structures. They may need help in unscrambling initials and professional jargon which simplify communication for professionals but obscure it for other people. Informal discussions with those involved may be helpful for this purpose.

■ **Organise training days** like those offered to members of joint care planning teams, but adapted to carers' particular needs. The voluntary sector can play a useful role here, organising a training day on participation in community health councils, joint consultative committees and client care planning teams. Experienced committee members might describe each body and discuss the problems of participation. Just such a day was held in Taunton by the regional officers of MIND, Mencap and Age Concern, together with the National Council for Voluntary Organisations. It attracted a number of people not already involved in such committees.

DEVELOPING POLICY

It may be helpful to draw together some principles for policy making in this area. Listed below are some suggestions which could be added to and amended to fit local circumstances. You may find it helpful to discuss these ideas with colleagues.

Policy statements

There should be a firm commitment to provide all services in partnership with carers. This means regular and genuine consultation, covering not only the nature and quantity of services but also their quality.

- Carers should be offered direct membership of service committees, planning groups and joint planning structures.
- Formal consultation should be supplemented by informal discussions with carers, including discussions with carers' groups and one-off consultations through meetings set up for this purpose.
- Surveys of carers can be particularly useful to gauge carers' reactions to individual services.

Organisation

Effective consultation means giving carers maximum opportunities to express their views to policy makers and planners. There is a dilemma in using carers' organisations because although they are a convenient means of finding carers, they may not always be representative, especially of black and ethnic minority carers. Effective consultation means:

- Supporting and developing informal carers' groups and carers' forums.
- Adapting planning structures to enable carers to play a fuller part.
- Providing carers with help to attend meetings, such as sitting and transport.
- Briefing and supporting carers who are involved in formal structures. This may be done by a carers' support worker, where such a post exists.
- Arranging informal meetings between carers (individually or through groups) and service providers.

Training

The involvement of carers in consultation may entail changes in the procedures followed, with committee meetings becoming less streamlined and more time-consuming.

- Those who sit on committees will need training to work with carers and some guidance to help them cope with the changed arrangements. Guidance about how to help carers on committees should also be available.
- Those carers who become involved in formal consultations should be offered some training in committee skills. They need specific information about the body in which they are involved and its relations to the wider decision-making process.

The Rochdale Carers' Day

In Rochdale, a Carers' Day focussing on health issues was organised by the local branch of the Carers' National Association with the help of the Health Education Unit. It aimed to provide information about carers' experiences and needs in a form that could be used by service planners. Prepared over several months and well publicised through posters and leaflets, the press, notices distributed by post offices along with pensions and directly by professionals in touch with carers, the day was attended by 150 carers. These expressed high levels of stress, anger and loneliness. As well as discussing health problems arising through caring, they made a number of practical suggestions about how their situation might be improved. These were subsequently incorporated into a Carers' Charter, with specific recommendations for local service providers; 500 copies of this have been sold throughout the country.

The charter brought dramatic gains in the recognition of carers within both the district health authority and the social services department. It was presented to the Joint Care Planning Team and two places for carers were subsequently granted on the JCPT. Carers have also been invited to join the social services Elderly Development Planning Team. Carers were also invited to talk to primary health care teams, planning teams for the elderly and trainee nurses, as well as senior managers of the district health authority. The social services department responded positively to a number of issues identified, for instance accepting the need to make respite care more accessible to carers in a crisis. Joint finance has also been obtained for the post of a carers' liaison adviser, to provide a contact point and advocate for carers. It is widely felt that these advances would have taken much longer to achieve without the Carers' Day.

CONCLUDING COMMENTS

We write, without question, at a difficult time. Service providers have a great deal on their individual and organisational agendas. Bookshelves are groaning with reports about policies and arrangements for community care. Most recent, and most pertinent, is the report by Sir Roy Griffiths, *Community Care: Agenda for Action*. This has made some major proposals for change, the status of which at the time of writing is unclear. If and when these proposals are implemented, they will radically alter the way services are organised, giving much greater emphasis to the need to support carers. Yet most of what is written here will continue to apply whatever the organisational arrangements for delivering community care. The basics of good local practice do not become out of date.

This book has been developed in a spirit of reason and common sense. It rests on a concern to be assertive of carers' needs, but not antagonistic to service providers nor unsympathetic to their particular problems and perspectives. Carers are not a clamouring crowd nor would they wish to be seen to be. The essence of family care is that it is provided with love and 'sharing without reckoning'; help is given where it is needed and as much as is needed. Carers, asking little for themselves, do not seek to make noisy demands.

The work of carers' organisations has greatly increased awareness of these issues among service providers as well as among the general public. Yet the need for change will become more and more pressing. The number of people needing care is growing fast, more evident in the case of very elderly people. At the same time, the supply of ready carers is diminishing. With the increasing participation of women in the labour force, questions arise about their continued willingness and ability to fulfil the traditional caring role. It can no longer be assumed that there is a sizeable supply of potential carers, sitting at home looking for something useful to do with their time.

Considerable attention is currently being given to these issues and their implications for services. What is being urged here is a strategy that takes account of carers' needs in these discussions. Local and health authorities cannot afford not to take carers into account. They need to focus on how existing services can best be modified to respond to carers' needs and views. Whatever the considerable pressures in other directions, the energies of planners, staff and all those who work in this field need to be turned to the positive issues of partnership with carers and partnership in care.

True partnership will stem from recognition. This underpins every other step that service providers will take. With due recognition, carers will be treated as equals, given information and support and consulted in the course of service planning and delivery. With recognition, they will be treated as people to work with, to whom practical problems and hitches can be explained. Most of all, with recognition, they will have their responses to both problems and services taken seriously.

One issue which needs to be noted here is the tension between undertaking 'projects' and getting good practice fed into mainstream services. Projects for carers are becoming increasingly common. These can do a great deal of good, especially where there is a committed worker involved. They help to set up new schemes and groups, make professionals more aware of what can be done and generally stir up local attention. On the other hand, they are time-limited, operate often in considerable isolation (both organisational and personal for the worker involved) and it can be argued that they marginalise services for carers by taking them out of the mainstream. It is partly, of course, a question of the amount of resources available and the amount of commitment given.

Another central issue is developing a teamwork approach. It can be difficult for professionals not only to work closely with carers but also to work closely with each other. Local integration is much more easily said than done, especially where individual professionals have their own internal organisational tensions and uncertainties. Sometimes a sense of common purpose can bind people together. So too can the realisation that time and resources can be saved through inter-professional cooperation in a particular area. But, on the whole, the necessary trust takes some time to develop. It simply will not happen overnight.

There is, at all levels, a need for a sense of purpose and vision. At the top, this means a commitment to take on difficult issues and bring about change. In the often unsung levels of middle management, it means recognising innovation and helping people to bring their ideas to fruition. For those working on the ground, it means feeling that there is an organisation behind them, encouraging them to seek out new ways of doing their job better. The changes may often be modest, but they can make a real difference to people's lives. The time for action is now.

SOME USEFUL ORGANISATIONS

Age Concern (England)
Bernard Sunley House
Pitcairn Road
Mitcham
Surrey CR4 3LL
(01) 640 5431

Alzheimers Disease Society
158/160 Balham High Street
London SW12 9BN
(01) 675 6557

Arthritis Care
6 Grosvenor Crescent
London SW1X 7ER
(01) 235 0902

Association of Crossroads Care Attendant Schemes
10 Regent Place
Rugby
Warwicks
CV21 2PN
(0788) 736353

Cancerlink
17 Britannia Street
London WC1X 9JN
(01) 833 2451

Cancer Relief Macmillan Fund
Anchor House
15/19 Britten Street
London SW3 3TY
(01) 351 7811

Carers' National Association
29 Chilworth Mews
London W2 3RG
(01) 724 7776

Chest, Heart and Stroke Association
Tavistock House North
Tavistock Square
London WC1H 9JE
(01) 387 3012

Contact a Family
16 Strutton Ground
London SW1P 2HP
(01) 222 2695

Counsel and Care for the Elderly
Twyman House
16 Bonny Street
London NW1 9LR
(01) 485 1566

Disability Alliance
Denmark Street
London WC2H 8NJ
(01) 240 0806

Downs Syndrome Association
12/13 Clapham Common Southside
London SW4 7AA
(01) 720 0008

Family Fund
PO Box 50
York YO1 1UY
(0904) 21115

Holiday Care Service
2 Old Bank Chambers
Station Road
Horley
Surrey RH6 9HW
(0293) 774535

MENCAP
Royal Society for Mentally Handicapped Children and Adults
123 Golden Lane
London EC1Y 0RT
(01) 253 9433

MIND
National Association for Mental Health
22 Harley Street
London W1N 2ED
(01) 637 0741

Multiple Sclerosis Society
25 Effie Road
Fulham
London SW6 1EE
(01) 736 6267

National Council for Voluntary Organisations
26 Bedford Square
London WC1B 3HU
(01) 636 4066

National Schizophrenia Fellowship
79 Victoria Road
Surbiton
Surrey KT6 4NS
(01) 390 3651

Parkinson's Disease Society
36 Portland Place
London W1N 3DG
(01) 323 1174

RADAR
Royal Association for Disability and Rehabilitation
25 Mortimer Street
London W1N 8AB
(01) 637 5400

Sense – the National Deaf-Blind and Rubella Association
311 Grays Inn Road
London WC1X 9PT
(01) 278 1005

The Spastics Society
12 Park Crescent
London W1N 4EQ
(01) 636 5020

Standing Conference of Ethnic Minority Senior Citizens
(SCEMSC)
5 Westminster Bridge Road
St Georges Circus
London SE1 7XW
(01) 928 0095

Terrence Higgins Trust
BM AIDS
London WC1N 3XX
(01) 831 0330

FURTHER READING

General Reading

Age Concern, *Residential Care – is it for me?* HMSO 1988

Allen, Isobel *Short Stay Residential Care for the Elderly* Policy Studies Institute 1983

Allen, Isobel et al *Informal Care Tomorrow* Policy Studies Institute 1987

Audit Commission *Making a Reality of Community Care* HMSO 1986

Baldwin, Sally *The Cost of Caring – families with disabled children* Routledge and Kegan Paul 1985

Bayley, Michael et al *Practising Community Care – developing locally based practice* Joint Unit for Social Services Research, University of Sheffield 1988

Briggs, Anna and Oliver, Judith *Caring – experiences of looking after disabled relatives* Routledge and Kegan Paul 1985

Connelly, Naomi *Care in the Multi-Racial Community* PSI Discussion Paper 20, 1988

DHSS *Care for a Change* 1987

DHSS *From Home Help to Home Care* 1987

Dant, Tim et al *Identifying, Assessing and Monitoring the Needs of Elderly People at Home* Project Paper, Open University/Policy Studies Institute 1987

Disability Alliance *Poverty and Disability – Breaking the Link – the case for a comprehensive disability income scheme* Disability Alliance

Finch, Janet *Give and Take – changing patterns of family obligations* Polity Press 1988

Finlay, Rosalind and Reynolds, Jill *Social Work and Refugees: a handbook on working with people in exile in the UK* National Extension College/Refugee Action 1987

Glendenning, Caroline *Unshared Care – parents and their disabled children* Routledge and Kegan Paul 1983

Greater London Association for the Disabled *All Change – a consumer study of public transport* GLAD 1986

Green, Hazel *Informal Carers – General Household Survey 1985, Supplement A* HMSO 1988

Griffiths, Sir Roy *Community Care – Agenda for Action – a report to the Secretary of State for Social Services* HMSO 1988

Hatch, Stephen and Hinton, Teresa *Self Help in Practice – a study of Contact a Family, community work and family support* University of Sheffield, 1986

Hedley, Rodney and Norman, Alison *Going Places – two experiments in voluntary transport* Centre for Policy on Ageing 1984

Jowell, Tessa and Bould, Martin *How to Succeed at Consultation* CareLink, No. 3, Winter 1987 (copies available from Informal Caring Support Unit, Kings Fund Centre)

Keeble, Ursula *Aids and Adaptations* Bedford Square Press 1978

Kellaher, Leonie et al *Living in Homes – a consumer view of old people's homes* BASE/CESSA 1985

Leat, Diana and Gay, Pat *Paying for Care – a study of policy and practice in paid care schemes* Policy Studies Institute 1987

Levin, Enid et al *The Supporters of Confused Elderly Persons at Home* National Institute for Social Work

Midwinter, Eric *Caring for Cash – the issue of private domiciliary care* Centre for Policy on Ageing 1986

National Audit Office *Community Care Developments* HMSO 1987

NAHA/NCVO Joint Working Party *Partnerships for Health* NAHA 1987

National Consumer Council *Good Advice for All – guidelines on standards for local advice services* National Consumer Council 1986

NCVO Joint Planning Working Group *A Stake in Planning – joint planning and the voluntary sector* Community Care Project 1986

NCVO Community Care Project *Voluntary Sector Forums on Community Care* NCVO 1987

NCVO Community Care Project *Practice Notes – developing voluntary sector participation in joint planning* 1987

Norman, Alison *Triple Jeopardy – growing old in a second homeland* Centre for Policy on Ageing, 1985

Oswin, Maureen *They Keep Going Away – a critical study of short-term residential care for children who are mentally handicapped* King Edwards Hospital Fund for London 1984

Parker, Gillian *With Due Care and Attention* Family Policy Studies Centre 1985

Richardson, Ann and Ritchie, Jane *Making the Break – parents' views about adults with a mental handicap leaving the parental home* King Edward's Hospital Fund for London 1986

Sheik, Samar 'An Asian Mothers' Self Help Group' in Ahmed, Shama et al (eds) *Social Work with Black Children and Their Families* Batsford 1986

Standing Conference of Ethnic Minority Senior Citizens *Ethnic Minority Senior Citizens – the question of policy* SCEMSC 1986

Tester, Sue and Meredith, Barbara Ill Informed? A study of information and support for elderly people in the inner city Policy Studies Institute 1987

Tooth, Jenny Partnership in Care – a strategy for the support of carers of frail elderly people Age Concern Greater London Health Forum 1987

Unell, Judith Help for Self Help Bedford Square Press 1986

Ungerson, Claire Policy is Personal – sex, gender and informal care Tavistock 1987

Wagner G Residential Care – the research reviewed HMSO 1988

Wicks, Malcolm Caring Costs – the Social Security implications Family Policy Studies Centre 1986

Training and Development Materials

Action for Carers – a guide to multi-disciplinary support at local level Kings Fund Informal Caring Programme 1988. Price £9.50 inc p & p. 10% discount on 10 or more copies.

Carers – a video assisted workshop for primary health care professionals supporting carers of elderly and disabled people ESCATA 1987. Price £80.00 inc. p & p

Shared Concern – breaking the news to parents that their newborn child has a disability Kings Fund Informal Caring Programme 1987. Price £50.00 inc p & p for video tape, 50 booklets and tutors guidelines.

These training materials are available from the Book Sales Department, Kings Fund Centre, 126 Albert Street, London NW1 7NF. Telephone: 01-267 6111. Payment with order.

Guides for Carers

Disability Alliance ERA Disability Rights Handbook – a guide to rights, benefits and services for all people with disabilities and their families (13th edition) Disability Alliance 1988. Available from Disability Alliance, 25 Denmark Street, London WC2H 8NJ. Price £3.50

Jee, Maggie Taking a Break – a guide for people caring at home Kings Fund Informal Caring Programme 1987. Available from Taking a Break, Newcastle-upon-Tyne X NE85 2AQ. Price – free to carers, £0.60 to others.

Kohner, Nancy Caring at Home – a handbook for people looking after someone at home National Extension College, 1988. Single copies available from Book Sales Department, Kings Fund Centre, 126 Albert Street, London NW1 7NF. Price £2.50 inc p & p. Bulk copies available from National Extension College, 18 Brooklands Avenue, Cambridge CB2 2HN.

Leicester CVS/SCOPE Niradharoki Dekhbhal/Asian Carers Video available from Leicester CVS, 32 de Montfort Street, Leicester LE1 7GD. Price £25.00.

Wilson, Judy Caring Together – guidelines for carers' self help and support groups National Extension College 1988. Available from Book Sales Department, Kings Fund Centre, 126 Albert Street, London NW1 7NF. Price £3.95 inc p & p.

DIRECTORY OF INITIATIVES

Listed alphabetically by the name of the organisation, project or location, as given in the text. Consult the index for page reference.

Every effort has been made to contact all the organisations mentioned in the text and to obtain correct details and permission to include them in this Directory of Initiatives. Unfortunately, the list is not comprehensive, and some information will become out of date as premises, funding or staff change.

Alzheimers Disease Society (Birmingham)
Care and Resource Centre
176 Soho Hill
Handsworth
Birmingham B19 1AF
Tel: 021 551 1016
Contact: Mrs Jenny Pitt

Alzheimers Disease Society (South Cleveland)
The Poplars
Holgate
St Barnabas Road
Middlesbrough TS5 6DZ
Tel: 0642 820921/2
Contact: The Organiser

ARMS (Action for Research into Multiple Sclerosis)
Head Office
4a Chapel Hill
Stansted
Essex CM24 3AG
Tel: 0279 815553

Multiple Sclerosis Counselling Service
London: 01 222 3123 (24 hr)
Scotland: 041 945 3939 (9 am - 11 pm)
Midlands: 021 476 4229 (9 am - 11 pm)

BACUP (British Asociation of Cancer United Patients and their families and friends)
121/123 Charterhouse Street
London EC1M 6AA
Tel: Cancer Information Service
01 608 1611

Berkshire Social Services
Shire Hall
Shinfield Park
Reading RG2 9XG
Tel: 0734 875444 x 4826
Contact: Heather Wing,
Principal Officer (Elderly & Physically Handicapped)

Bexley Community Care Scheme
London Borough of Bexley
Social Services Department
Civic Offices
The Broadway
Bexleyheath
Kent DA6 7LB
Contact: Nan Maitland

Birmingham Multi-Handicap Group
1a Cleveland Tower
Holloway Head
Birmingham B1 1UB
Tel: 021 643 5948
Contact: Mrs Susanna McCorry

Boots Co plc
Health Care Business Centre
Nottingham NG2 3AA
Contact: Boots Occupational Therapist

The catalogue of aids and equipment is available free from all branches of Boots

Bradford Social Services Department
Elderly Sitting Service and Elderly Placement Scheme
Pennine House
39 Well Street
Bradford BD1 5RE
Tel: 0274 752918
Contact: Richard Kennedy or Sid Yelland

Brent Triangle
120 Craven Park Road
London NW10 8QD
Tel: 01 965 4371
Contact: Steven Attwood, Coordinator

Bristol – patient participation
Whiteladies Health Centre
Carers Support Group
44 Harcourt Road
Redlands
Bristol BS6 7RE
Tel: 0272 245803
Contact: Margaret Hanstead

British Red Cross (London Branch)
3 Grosvenor Crescent
London SW1X 7EG
Tel: 01 235 3241 x 150
Contact: Miss Jackie Knight,
Social Service Adviser

CancerLink
17 Brittania Street
London WC1X 9JN
Tel: 01 833 2451

Care Alternatives Ltd
206 Worple Road
Wimbledon
London SW20 8PN
Contact: Lucianne Sawyer

*Also four branches covering
Cambridge, Exeter, Portsmouth and
Isle of Wight, and Hertfordshire and
Essex.*

**Care for Elderly People at
Home Project**
Gloucester Health Authority
Rikenel
Montepelier
Gloucester GL1 1LY
Tel: 0452 29421 x 279/285
Contact: Tim Dant or Judith Gill

C A R E S
The Church of the Good
Shepherd
4 Bromford Lane
West Bromwich
West Midlands B70 7HP
Tel: 021 553 0190
Contact: Mrs Cooke

Caring Together
c/o Signpost Stockport or
Stockport CVS
(*see separate entries*)

**CHOICE – The Case
Management Service**
152 Camden Road
London NW1 9HL
Tel: 01 482 3687
Contact: Penny Banks and
Vivien Kerr

Contact a Family
16 Strutton Ground
London SW1P 2HP
Tel: 01 222 2695
Contact: Carol Youngs,
National Development Officer

**Darlington Health
Authority**
Community Unit Archer Street
Darlington DL3 6LT
Tel: 0325 465218
Contact: Dr Malcolm Stone

Dial-a-Ride contact
London Dial-a-Ride Users
Association
25 Leighton Road
London NW5 2QD
Tel: 01 482 2325
Contact: The Director

Disability Alliance
25 Denmark Street
London WC2H 8NJ

Docklands Light Railway
*A leaflet entitled 'Access to the
Docklands Light Railway' is available
from*
Disabled Passengers Unit
London Regional Transport
55 Broadway
London SW1H 0BB
Tel: 01 222 5600
Contact: John Bull

FACE/STOP Scheme
Social Services Dept
Civic Centre
Newcastle upon Tyne NE1 8PA
Tel: 091 232 8520
Contact: Norman Hodgson,
Principal Assistant Adult
Services

Family Support Unit
Eastbourne Lodge
5 Eastbourne Road
Middlesbrough
Cleveland TS5 6QS
Tel: 0642 820000
Contact: Rev. Michael Wright

**Haringey Mental Health
Relative Support
Association**
London Borough of Haringey
Social Services Area 2
72 Lawrence Road
London N15 4ES
Tel: 01 809 4466 x 137
Contact: Mike Zamora

The Hillside Centre
Station Road
Plympton
Plymouth
Devon PL7 3AZ
Tel: 0752 330261
Contact: Mr Ian Jane, Manager

Hove Carers Centre
210 Church Road
Hove BN3 2DJ
Tel: 0273 207879
Contact: The Coordinator

**Hull Council for Voluntary
Service**
29 Anlaby Road
Hull HU1 2PG
Tel: 0482 24474
Contact: Lesley Hepworth,
Carers Support Worker

**ICAN Asian Family
Support Centre**
176 Windmill Lane
Smethwick
Warley
West Midlands B66 3NA
Tel: 021 558 2198
Contact: Jan Uppal

**In Safe Hands, Age
Concern York**
70 Walmgate
York YO1 2TL
Tel: 0904 627995/621020
Contact: Margaret Sharp

**Information for Carers
Project**
Citizens Advice Bureau
Hill House
Bishopsford Road
Morden
Surrey SM4 6BL
Te: 01 648 1209
Contact: Alison Ramdas

**Kent Community Care
Centre**
Cairn Ryan Day Hospital
101 London Road
Kearsney
Dover CT16 3AA
Tel: 0304 824144
Contact: Robin Saunders,
Senior Social Worker

Leeds City Council
Family Placement Scheme
Voluntary and Advisory
Services
Social Services Department
Sweet Street
Leeds LS11 9DQ
Tel: 0532 463401
Contact: Assistant Director

Leeds City Council
Social Services Department
229 Woodhouse Lane
Leeds LS2 9LF
Tel: 0532 448921
Contact: Bill Walton

Leicester Carers Forum
c/o Leicester Council for
Voluntary Service (*see below*)

**Leicester Council for
Voluntary Service**
32 de Montfort Street
Leicester LE1 7GD
Tel: 0533 555600
Contact: Shirley Duddy,
Community Resources Officer

Leicester Rights Centre
Alliance House
6 Bishop Street
Leicester LE1 6AD
Tel: 0533 553781
Contact: Gill Gardner

**Lewisham Carers
Handbook**
Women's Equality Unit
London Borough of Lewisham
Town Hall
Catford
London SE6 4RU
Tel: 01 695 6000

**Liverpool Branch of
Carers National
Association**
38 Borrowdale Road
Liverpool L15 3LE
Tel: 051 523 8855
Contact: Mary Dixon

Multiple Sclerosis Society
25 Effie Road
Fulham
London SW6 1EE
Tel: 01 381 4022
Contact: The Welfare
Department

Neighbourhood Care Project
47/48 Fleet Street
Swindon
Wilts SN1 1RE
Tel: 0793 618558 (24 hour ansaphone)
Contact: Debbie Bignall, Project Worker

Nottingham Community Mental Handicap Teams
Ashbourne House
49/51 Forest Road East
Nottingham NG1 4HT
Tel: 0602 413707
Contact: Martin Jackaman

Oldham Health Authority
Department of Community Medicine
6th Floor
St Peter House
Oldham OL1 1JY
Tel: 061 624 0544
Contact: Stephen Watkins

Oldham Social Services Department
13th Floor
Civic Centre
West Street
Oldham OL1 1UW
Contact: Mrs B Beeden

Options Family Support Service (NCH in Wales)
St Davids Court
68a Cambridge Road East
Cardiff CF1 9DW
Tel: 0222 222127
Contact: Joan Williams

The Pepperpot Club
Community Centre
2nd Floor, 39/41 Acklam Road
Ladbroke Grove
London W10 5RD
Tel: 01 968 6940
Contact: Euline Walcot

Rochdale Branch of Carers National Association
36 Severn Road
Heywood
Lancs OL10 4RY
Tel: 0706 65482
Contact: Vera Mearns, Secretary

SCOPE
Belgrave Neighbourhood Centre
Rothley Street
Leicester LE4 6AF
Tel: 0533 681638
Contact: Mr P Lakhani

Scottish Council for Single Parents
Sitter Services
13 Gayfield Square
Edinburgh EH1 3NX
Tel: 031 557 3121
Contact: Project Leader

Sense
311 Grays Inn Road
London WC1X 8PT
Tel: 01 278 1005
Contact: Information Officer

Signpost Stockport
Torkington Centre
Torkington Road
Stockport SK7 4PY
Tel: 061 483 0884
Contact: Linda Pike/Eileen Stirland

Southall Contact a Family
St George's Church
1 Lancaster Road
Southall
Middlesex UB1 1NP
Tel: 01 571 6381
Contact: Hardeesh Rai

Stockport CVS
Russell Morley House
8/16 Lower Hill Gate
Stockport SK1 1JE
Tel: 061 477 0246
Contact: Shirley Best

Sutton Carers Project
Sutton Social Services
Civic Offices
St Nicholas Way
Sutton SM1 1EA
Contact: Anne Pinchin

Tameside Carers Survey
Policy Research Unit
Policy Services Department
Tameside Metropolitan
Borough Council
Council Offices
Wellington Road
Ashton under Lyne
Greater Manchester OL6 6DL
Tel: 051 330 8355
Contact: Alex O'Neil

Wallasey Carers Centre
The Place in the Park
Central Park
off Liscard Road
Wallasey
Merseyside L44
Contact: George Burkey

INDEX

Addresses of projects may be found in the Directory of Initiatives.

KING ALFRED'S COLLEGE
LIBRARY